Praise for *Nunc Coepi*

In *Nunc Coepi*, John "JT" Williams has written a powerful treatise. This is a story the world not only deserves to hear, but also *needs* to hear.

JT has been able to gloss over and make light of some of the more frightening aspects of his life when he relates his stories to his friends. In truth, it is beyond notable; I would more properly call it bravery. Thank you for sharing these intimate stories.

Just as Te-Nehisi Coates has written an amazing love letter to his son about how to live a life while Black—*Between the World and Me*—your boys deserve a permanent record of what their father has accomplished under extremely egregious circumstances growing up Black in Chicagoland.

JT has documented his experiences for every white person who professes liberalism but has no clue about the true cost of racism to the average minority individual.

This compendium is a kick in the ass of nearly every white who grows up privileged by color but does not recognize the advantage afforded them.

These recollections of a man to whom the world has not been kind, and yet has overcome, is a most powerful description of the resilience of the human spirit and is exceedingly difficult to refute or ignore. You are that man, JT.

—Roger Kay, author of *A Life Well Lived*

NUNC COEPI

— *Now I Begin* —

A Memoir

John T. Williams
San Diego, California

ISBN: 979-8-218-66234-9

LCCN: 2025908063

Printed in the United States of America

Acknowledgments

I struggled with this manuscript, including the decision to even pursue this task. It's been years in the making.

I will be forever grateful to Roger Kay for encouraging me to continue. I also appreciate Kris Martinsek for supporting Roger as they both pushed me to complete this writing.

In addition, I want to thank my sons (Ryan and Scott) for the joy and focus they have given me in my life.

There is a special thanks I give to my wife, Lady Jane, for her everlasting support and direction.

Finally, I want to thank Larry Edwards, my editor. His guidance was invaluable.

For various reasons, it is not possible to tell
the whole story of my life.
The following is only a thimbleful of events.

CONTENTS

My People

- Bertha—my mother, daughter of Viola Bailey
- Edward Gordon Williams—my "sire"
- John Williams—my grandfather, father to Edward (sire)
- Jane Holmes—my G-G-G-grandmother, born a *slave* on a plantation in Greenville, South Carolina, circa 1850
- Hanah Holmes—my G-G-grandmother, daughter of Jane Holmes, mother of Janie Roman
- Janie Roman—great-grandmother, aka Big Momma, daughter of Hanna Holmes, born in 1885 in South Carolina
- Viola Bailey—my grandmother, daughter of Janie Roman, sisters to Gladys and Sarah
- Monroe Williams—my uncle, son of Viola Bailey, brother of Bertha Miner, stepson of Alex Bailey
- Thad Williams—my cousin, son of Monroe Williams
- Jesse Miner—my stepfather,
- Michael Miner—my stepbrother, son of Jesse Miner
- Savanah—tough girl at high school
- Charles Ballard—fought Junior Jones
- Kim—first girlfriend
- McBride—college friend
- Henry Dent—roommate
- Jane—my wife
- Ryan Williams—my son, law professor
- Scott Williams—my son, entrepreneur
- Jonas Shaner—my stepson, registered nurse
- Luke Shaner—my stepson, architect

NUNC COEPI

– *Now I Begin* –

CHAPTER 1

My Sire

ONE EVENING, MOM AND I WERE HOME ALONE IN OUR HOME IN Portsmouth, Virginia. We heard a knock on the door. As Mom opened the door, a strange man shoved a gun through the opening and tried to push his way into our home.

I was three years old, almost four, and I recall this incident vividly, the details seared forever in my memory.

Mom slammed the door on his hand, but in addition to his hand he had inserted his foot in the door frame. This prevented the door from closing. However, he couldn't enter the home either because she had her entire weight against the door.

My mother screamed at the top of her lungs and began crying, ordering the man to leave.

My mother continued to scream at the top of her lungs and cry. I knew something was catastrophically wrong. Mom was also calling for her mother, my grandmother, to come to our aid. Even in that god-awful moment, I thought this was strange. My grandmother was in Chicagoland and nowhere near Virginia. I didn't understand the psychological trauma a person can suffer under extreme duress.

Think, a wounded soldier, lying on the battlefield, screaming in pain, dying, calling for his mother in desperation.

After what seemed an eternity, the man extricated himself and left.

Later that evening, Edward—my "Sire," Mom's husband—returned home. Mom was still upset and near hysteria. He asked her to calm down and describe the man. At first, she couldn't. Finally, she composed herself enough to give a description of the intruder.

Edward slowly rose from his seat and went into their bedroom. He opened the closet door, placed his hand on the right side of a top shelf, and retrieved a gun.

I had followed him into their bedroom. To this day, I don't know why I followed him. We had never had much interaction. In fact, he had made it clear he didn't want me following him around. Further, he made doubly sure I never knew where he kept his gun. But for some reason, this situation struck me as being different, more important than our daily existence.

While I watched, huddled in the doorway to the room, he strapped up his "Roscoe," a small revolver also known as a "wheel gun."

I also noticed he didn't change into his Navy dress-white Shore Patrol uniform. He remained in his street clothes, with a light overcoat covering the gun.

Two days later, he returned home. I again followed him into their bedroom. Edward removed the gun and holster, which he returned to the righthand side of the top shelf in their closet.

He said nothing. Mom never discussed the incident. I don't know for sure what happened.

All I know is no one ever tried to breach our threshold again.

My Sire was a *BAD* man.

I called Edward my sire and not my father or dad.

Why? The answer is simple. Edward was part of a transaction that brought me into this world. That event didn't make him my "father," and it damn sure didn't make him my daddy!

However, that event did have a lasting effect on how I viewed the world around me. It foretold a life that included violence and street justice and a dash of humility.

Thus, my life began.

CHAPTER 2

Lineage

I CAN TRACE MY LINE BACK TO A LADY NAMED JANE. I WILL call her Jane Holmes. This lady was my great-grandmother's grandmother.

Jane Holmes was born a slave on a plantation in Greenville, South Carolina. Yes, born a slave but lived to see freedom. Jane Holmes didn't work in the fields; rather, she worked in the big house as a cook. I find it mildly interesting that my wife is named Jane, as was my great grandmother, also named Jane. My great grandmother's birth certificate gives her name as Anna Janie Thompkins. We always called her Janie Roman.

Family oral history describes Jane Holmes, the slave, as a big woman some six feet in height, powerfully built, and one of the best cooks in the South. This lady was brown skin in color, which means her father was one of the white men from the plantation. She lived to be 100 years old and bore several children.

One of her children was a girl named Hanah, a petite, brown-skinned woman who bore several children of her own. However, she only lived to be 18 years old before dying in childbirth with her last child. That last child was my great-grandmother, Janie Roman.

My great-grandmother married a man whose last name was

Roman. We called her Big Momma. She stood 5'10" tall, had brown skin, sported a long, thick mane of hair, and was full-bodied. Strong in her physical person, tough mentally, and had an iron will. Further, she had an unshakable sense of right and wrong. She had three children, all girls: Gladys, Sarah, and Viola.

Viola was my mother's mother and my Grandmother; Gladys and Sarah were my mother's aunts. This made Gladys and Sarah my great-aunts. They mirrored their mother, Big Momma, in that they were physically tall, brown-skinned women.

Viola apparently had a different father. She too was physically tall and strong and had a head full of long, straight hair but was dark skinned. Viola was also a handful. She feared nothing. For example, somehow the family migrated from South Carolina to the Chicago, Illinois area (Evanston). I'm not sure why this took place or what was the catalyst. I can only assume they sought greater opportunities for themselves and their children. I do know they made the move during the Roaring Twenties.

During this time, also known as the Prohibition Era, after alcoholic beverages had been banned, Viola found work with a crew making bathtub gin. They sold this illegal booze in Chicago. Despite the danger from other small-time bootleg outfits, and the risk posed by the law, Grandma adopted the attitude of "authorities and other outlaws be dammed."

Viola, like her mother, had multiple children, some while she was married, some when she was not. In addition to my mother, Viola had three other children: Etta Ruth, Janie, and Monroe. Etta and Janie were my aunts, Monroe my uncle.

Aunt Etta married and became Etta Hilliard; her sister Janie married and became Janie Bowman, and Monroe kept his last name. Thus, he remained Monroe Williams.

My Grandmother Viola married a man with the last name of Williams. However, she wasn't married to the man named Williams when my mother was conceived. In fact, Viola wasn't married at all. My mother, Bertha, was born out of wedlock. A childhood photo depicts her as a small, dark-skinned girl with very short hair.

My mother was given the last name Williams. She in turn married a man whose last name happened to be Williams, one Edward Gordon Williams. My mother was a Williams who married a Williams.

Bertha

As a small girl, Mom had a very hard life growing up in Evanston. Others teased her for being so small, having very short hair, and being born without knowing her father. My mother never knew her father's name, and Viola would never tell.

Mom developed a complex early on and always said she was "slow." In school, Mom was in special education (designed for mentally challenged children). As a member of the "special education class," her classmates teased her even more. Nevertheless, Mom takes pride in the fact she learned how to read and write, and that she made it through eighth grade. She did start her freshman year in high school but dropped out before finishing ninth grade. Her troubled childhood and lack of education haunted her all her life. In referring to her mental state, Mom's mantra was "Johnny, I am slow."

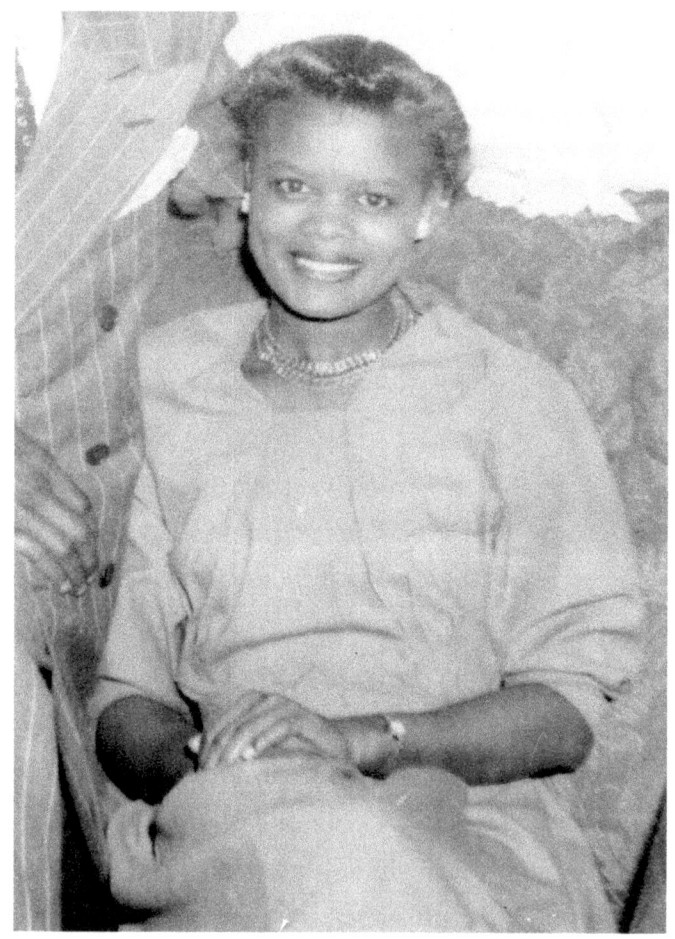

Bertha—my mother, daughter of Viola Bailey—
in her early twenties

Bertha-in her 80s

Janie Roman—great-grandmother, aka Big Momma, daughter of Hanna Holmes, born in 1885 in South Carolina

Viola Bailey at age 100—my grandmother, daughter of Janie Roman, sisters to Gladys and Sarah

Great Aunt Sarah

Monroe Williams—my uncle, son of Viola Bailey,
brother of Bertha Miner, stepson of Alex Bailey

Monroe Williams—7 years old

Jesse Miner—my stepfather

Jane—my wife—and me

JOHN WILLIAMS, Evanston's 5-10, 187-pound senior guard who helped Wildkits to another Suburban league championship this season. Williams is 1 of 5 guards named to All-State squad.

John T Williams working construction—19 years old

John T and Jane—at their wedding

Ryan Williams — my son, law professor

Scott Williams — my son, entrepreneur

Jonas Shaner— my stepson, registered nurse

Luke Shaner — my stepson, architect

CHAPTER 3

The Baby Years and Hard Times

I was born in the Chicagoland area of Evanston, Illinois in 1949. When I was six months old, my mother and the man she married—Edward Gordon Williams, my "sire"—moved to Portsmouth, Virginia. We lived in a clapboard shanty of a house among other houses of the same style and structure in an all-black neighborhood.

Edward periodically found himself in trouble of one type or another, and his solution was to join (and rejoin) the military. Specifically, the Military Police. He became a member of the U.S. Navy's Shore Patrol. Interestingly, most members were armed only with a baton. He carried both a baton and a Roscoe, a small revolver.

My sire left my mom when I was two years old, came back when I was three, left again (for good this time) when I was four.

Later in life, my aunts described how he and his other black Shore Patrol brethren would flow through the middle of a black night club. The very tough men in the club would part. They did so reluctantly, but part they did.

Due to Edward's personality (and perhaps his vocation . . . no, it was his personality) he made a number of serious enemies.

Adolescent Years and More Hard Times

About a year later, after I had turned five, my Great-aunt Sarah arrived in Portsmouth to take me back to Illinois. We rode the train from Virginia to Chicago, and from there to Evanston via the L (Chicago's elevated train).

A few days later, Sarah returned with me to the Chicago train station to meet my mother, Bertha. I remember distinctly looking past Mom and saying, "Where is he?"

Mom had a strange look in her eye, and she said, "He's not coming."

And he never did. I never saw Edward again, nor did I ever hear from him or about him. All I know is that he was born in Alabama and that his father, my grandfather, was named John.

My mother did tell me I was physically similar to John, my grandfather. When my mother first met him, he was big, strong, and an old man. Interestingly, he did have a young wife who was "high yellow," a very light-skinned black woman.

Other than these few facts, I know almost nothing about Edward or his side of the family.

There are no words to describe how hard things were for Mom and me. She had a mother and grandmother, who were my grandmother and great-grandmother, but they were fighting their own battles to survive.

My mom was a black woman in her twenties, with a five-year-old child; she had only an eighth-grade education, no real skill set, no husband, and lived in Chicagoland.

I have heard people complain about growing up in a household having to share the bathroom with multiple siblings. Try sharing a bathroom with various people from multiple, unrelated families. People whose attitudes regarding hygiene varied.

Once, we lived in a very large, run-down building that contained so many different families it was known as the "Beehive."

Mom couldn't afford our own apartment, thus we sub-rented a room inside another family's small apartment in the Hive. The entire apartment was small, dark, and not overly clean. We shared a refrigerator with the lady whose apartment we shared. She had a thief for a son— basically, an all-around bad individual. I vividly remember a piece of our cheese in the refrigerator with dirt from his fingers. He stole a portion of the cheese and left his telltale marks. He would later spend much of his time in reform school, with prison sentences as his next stops.

The Beehive was not a good place.

The euphemism used for the young men in the Hive that went away to "summer school" meant they were incarcerated. Their "summer school" was in fact reform school—a system used to house juvenile offenders. All too many black men began a life of crime in their youth, which included our landlady's son.

However, the worst place we lived was in another facility. The bathroom and kitchen were shared with several other families. It had a "room" that was a screened-in porch. There were no permanent walls, no heat, and we lived and slept there year-round, including the brutal winter months.

In those days, the Chicago winters were 10 to 20 degrees below zero on a routine basis.

I have trouble describing the "Hawk" or "Hawkins," African American vernacular for what we called the cold blustery wind that blew in from Lake Michigan, truly a cruel invention by God. The hawk reference equates the strong winds to how fast a hawk flies and the biting cold to the bird's sharp talons.

Winter nights, sleeping on that screened-in porch, chilled us to the bone thanks to the unforgiving and merciless Hawk. On those nights, we would say "The Hawk talks."

The *Chicago Defender*, on October 20, 1936, described it as "these cold mornings are on us—in other words 'Hawkins' has got us."

In the 1967 song, "Dead End Street," Chicago native Lou Rawls speaks the following intro:

> *I was born in a city that they call*
> *"The Windy City"*
> *They call it The Windy City because of "the Hawk"*
> *The Hawk*
> *The Almighty Hawk*
> *Mr. Wind*
> *Takes care of plenty of business 'round winter time*

It is also referenced in the first line of the Steve Goodman song, "A Dying Cub Fan's Last Request":

By the shores of old Lake Michigan
Where the Hawk Wind blows so cold

Mom worked incredibly hard. She cleaned houses, cooked, and worked in a laundry, long hours, long days. She had no vacation. We owned no car, or television, nor radio for that matter.

Once, when I was six years old, Mom and I were walking in the snow. The cold had become unbearable. I raised my arms saying, "Carry me."
She refused, saying, "Johnny, I have to walk, and you will too."

Mom had no health insurance. If she became sick, she couldn't work, which meant no income.

When I was seven, I started getting into rock fights with

other kids. It wasn't necessarily malicious; it was simply a game we played in the alley behind the dwelling where we lived. The alley was dirt and littered with broken glass, rocks, and other debris. In later years, we lived at another location where the city had paved the alley. We couldn't believe our luck. An alley that was paved with concrete rather than covered in dirt. What good fortune.

In any case, Mom said to me, "Stop throwing rocks. If you get hurt, I have no money for a doctor."

Guess what?

I was hit in my right eye with a rock. When I got home, Mom spanked me, placed some Vaseline on the eye, and told me to shut up and stop crying.

Rock fights, in play or anger, fist fights—it was something we did on a routine basis, including Mom.

One day, when Mom worked at Neilson's Laundry, she and another young black woman got into a fist fight. They were both so injured neither could work for two days.

That meant lost wages for them both.

If we had a problem with someone, we didn't spend much time discussing the "issues." Knock the offender on their butt right now. That was our approach.

Also, calling the police (while it did happen) was never a good idea.

I became a latchkey kid. By age eight, I walked home from school alone or with schoolmates. I let myself in to our "home." It would be wintertime dark, and the small place would be empty. Mom was at work. I made my supper, completed my chores, and finished my homework.

Things were hard, and without my Grandmother Viola and

Great-grandmother Big Momma, my mother and I would not have made it.

Grandma

My Grandmother Viola at one point was married to a man whose last name was Bailey. She had a son named Monroe from a previous marriage, my mom's older brother. When Monroe was a teenager, long before I was born, Bailey became angry with him and they fought.

Not arguing. They fought with their fists.

Grandma didn't say a thing because Bailey should have known not to beat his stepson, grandma's first-born child.

Grandma, in addition to her other talents, was a seamstress. She stabbed Bailey in the back with a pair of large scissors. She just missed his heart and almost killed him. Now for that one the police arrived. My grandmother was placed in jail. She didn't stay long. Bailey declined to press charges.

Bailey and Monroe fought no more.

Big Momma

Janie Roman, my great-grandmother. She told me stories about how as a child her family would get word the Ku Klux Klan in South Carolina was riding on a given night. On those nights, the people moved their few valuable possessions that were breakable to the floor. Then they would lie on the floor next to these possessions and wait.

At some point, the Klan rode up on their horses. Taking out their guns, the Klan shot into the people's cabins. This was during the late 1800s. The victims could do nothing because they were black and living in the South. They would lie on the floor, scared and praying the Klan's men would be content with staying outside while their bullets flew inside.

Then, in the aftermath, my people would rise, clean up the mess, and prepare to work the next day. Work for white people.

Big Momma, like the rest of the women in our family, was a domestic working for white people. Big Momma never liked white people.

More than once she told me, "Treat all white people with a long-handled spoon, You should be polite but don't get too close to them. White people will only hurt you."

I agreed with her but with a slight variation on that philosophy. I felt (and still do) all people should be treated with a long-handled spoon. I have never been impressed with the race of mankind.

Big Momma was a pipe-smoking woman who found a way of dealing with virtually every problem. For example, as she aged there were instances where she had trouble breathing as she slept. During this time, I read that as people got older, their circulation slowed when they slept. Thus, their lungs wouldn't work properly.

Big Momma felt it wasn't a matter of poor circulation. She would tell me, "Johnny, last night the witches were riding me." Hence, the trouble with her breathing.

Her solution?

The next night she would drink a shot of high-proof whiskey before bedtime and put her butcher knife under her pillow. Upon which she slept soundly.

In the morning, she swore the butcher knife kept the witches from riding her.

Even though I was only 11 years old at the time, I didn't

believe the butcher knife made a difference. It was the whiskey that improved her circulation.

However, I learned early on not to argue with a pipe-smoking black woman who carried a butcher knife and drank her whiskey straight.

Big Momma died of a stroke in 1965 when I was 16 years old. At this writing, I am 76 years old, and that was the first and last time I cried in public. I still grieve for the woman.

Teenage Years and Hard Times

As I approached my teens, my mom remarried after several years of being alone. She married a man named Jesse Miner, and he became my stepfather. Jesse was a good man, and he lived until 2017. He was born in South Carolina, the youngest of 13 children, and his parents were sharecroppers.

Jesse never learned to read or write. To say that placed tremendous limitations on his life (and therefore our lives) is an understatement. Reading and writing weren't skills that were considered important to many black people in the South in the early to mid-1900s.

Jesse was married once before. The dwelling where he lived with his previous wife was destroyed in a gas-line explosion, killing Jesse's first wife.

He did receive a bit of money, which he used to buy a townhouse in Evanston. It was only two bedrooms and one bathroom, but it was ours. Mom, Big Momma, Jesse, Jesse's son from his first marriage (Michael), and I all lived in this two-bedroom home.

After Big Momma died, my grandmother Viola Bailey needed a place to stay, so she moved in with us. My grandmother died in 2011, after living to be 101 years old.

Jesse could grow anything. We had a rather large backyard in Evanston, and Jesse grew corn, tomatoes, beans etc., and we had pears from our pear tree.

The thing that amazed me the most about this man was he remembered everything. He couldn't read or write so he learned to depend on his memory. A memory that was flawless.

Our lives were incredibly hard but extremely simple. Mom was afraid to drive, and Jesse couldn't read, and we had no money, so we had no car.

After years of odd jobs, Jesse obtained a position as a cook at Elder Hall for Northwestern University. He worked there for over 25 years.

My grandmother was a domestic and seamstress, Mom worked as a domestic, and I had my paper route, Big Momma raised me. I worked, went to school, ran the streets, entertained women and eventually played sports. That was my life.

Our lives were simple, structured, unimaginative, and hard. There wasn't time for reflection, or daydreaming. There was only the task at hand and what came next. There was very little wasted motion.

We got our first car when my Uncle Howard gave me an old beater when I turned 16. He was the husband of my Great-aunt Gladys. Mom had told me stories about how as a baby my uncle would have me stand on my own in his hand. His hands were big, and I was small. Perhaps this is where we bonded.

As Uncle Howard handed me the keys to the car, I felt grateful and humble. He was not obligated to do it. It was a maroon 1953 Chevy convertible, two doors. Due to rust, it had holes in the floorboards and a door that wouldn't close properly. However, it was mine. I named her Judy, and she was a lady.

Thus, when we wanted to travel, I drove to the given destination. Prior to that, we walked, or rode the bus, or traveled via the Chicago L—the rapid transit system. Or the other option was to follow Big Momma's advice: "Keep your black ass at home."

Great Aunt Sarah

One day when I was in my early teens, out of the blue my Great-aunt Sarah said she wanted to talk to me. She then told me the following story.

During the days when this country expanded westward, the railroads played an important part in that expansion. Several men, including black men, by then freed slaves, worked for the railroads.

She told me I had a relative from South Carolina who traveled out west to work on the railroads. Let's call him Jim.

One day Jim looked up and Harry, his neighbor from South Carolina, approached him. Jim was surprised and asked Harry what he was doing so far from home.

Harry, with a heavy heart, told Jim that he had to track him down to give him some bad news. Jim's wife, Mary, was cheating on him with a neighbor named George. Every Wednesday, like clockwork, George would visit Mary in her home (Jim's home) for sex.

Jim walked off the job that day and traveled with Harry back to South Carolina. Jim timed his arrival for a Wednesday. That evening, he entered his home and, sure enough, George was in bed with Mary.

Jim had armed himself with a shotgun. Upon seeing Jim, Mary and George jumped out of bed. Jim told Mary to stay out of the bed and told George to remain in the bed.

Jim then calmly shot George in the chest, killing him instantly. Mary screamed and ran from the room. Eventually, the white sheriff and a posse arrived and by then it was full-on night.

The sheriff asked Jim what had happened. Jim, without hesitation, told the sheriff that he'd just murdered a man he caught sleeping with his wife, Mary.

Aunt Sarah said, "Johnny, in them days things were done differently."

She explained that the sheriff told Jim, "You must be punished for the murder."

The punishment? Jim would have to dig a grave and bury George.

Jim said, "Fine." He loaded the body in the back of a wagon and drove into the woods. He dug the grave while the sheriff and his posse held torches and watched. Jim dumped the body in the grave, covered it up, and that was the end of the law's involvement.

Aunt Sarah then said, "For the next 25 years, Jim and Mary remained married. For all those years Jim made Mary sleep on that same bloody mattress and on those same bloody pillows. Mary never cheated on Jim again."

Then Aunt Sarah looked me in the eye and said, "Johnny, these are your people."

She then left the room and went home.

I learned certain principles from my family that have guided me all my life. "Walk softly but carry a big stick." One should be polite, give others the benefit of the doubt, be almost humble in nature.

However, when it's obvious a man is disrespecting you in the extreme, then without hesitation tear off his balls and pound them between his cheeks. Or give him a shotgun blast to the chest.

You cannot allow a man to **TOUCH** your pride.

A simple, unwavering, straightforward philosophy of life.

Other Lessons Learned from My People

Jesse was forced to rely on his memory due to his inability to read or write. I also learned to trust my memory. To accomplish this feat early on, I realized I must pay attention to the world around me.

When someone is speaking, for example, focus on what they are saying, not on what you plan on saying in response.

Mom taught me responsibility. If you have a task, then complete that task. This was particularly true if other people were depending upon you.

Grandma taught me never, ever back up or back down from a fight. Whether the fight was mental or physical.

Big Momma was more philosophical in nature. She taught me to think before I spoke. Also, if I had nothing to say, why say it?

To this day I don't care for people who chatter constantly about nothing of importance.

Big Momma told me, "Johnny you worry too much about things you can't fix. Don't worry about the mule going blind. Just sit up there and shake the lines."

They all taught me about honor, truthfulness, integrity, and a man should have a certain amount of physical courage.

Chapter 4

Evanston, Illinois

EVANSTON WAS TRULY A "TALE OF TWO CITIES." WEALTHY WHITE people on one side of town, the poor blacks on the other. Our family was in the working poor category. Although, no one we knew chose to collect welfare on a long-term basis. It was embarrassing.

False pride?

We worked. We worked harder than one could imagine. Catering to the needs of the wealthy white society on Chicago's North Shore.

There was no withholding for Social Security, pensions were unheard of, and we lived day by day.

There was one exception. Northwestern University did pay Jesse a decent wage and provided him with health insurance and a pension. As mentioned earlier, Jesse was a cook at Northwestern's Elder Hall. He prepared meals for hundreds of young men on a daily basis. He couldn't read; therefore, all those recipes he knew by heart, and he was an excellent cook. After he retired, Jesse's pension helped support my elderly mother.

Thank you, Northwestern University.

The Tale of Two Cities also extended to our black neighborhoods. Black people would fight each other and upon occasion kill each other. By the same token, if the neighborhood only had one potato and there was hunger, we all shared that potato.

Although hunger was rarely a problem. Our elders were farmers by training and gift. Momma Gaines shared the cherries from her cherry tree, Miss Ruth Heard shared her homemade jelly made from the grapes she grew on a patch of land in her yard.

We had a pear tree in our backyard, and we shared the fruit with the neighborhood.

Young bloods, including me, shoveled the snow for the elderly (no charge).

Despite the episodes of violence, we were an all-black neighborhood. An all-black family.

Violence

Certain of us are well schooled in the art of violence and mayhem. This is due to environment, temperament, desire, and skill set.

Violence was as much a part of our lives as breathing. At an early age, my grandmother told me never to start a fight but to always finish one. When we say fight, we don't mean verbal argument. Our definition of fight is a street fight: fists, knives, broken glass from the street, whatever weapon was handy.

Violence was so casual we didn't give it much thought. It was a way to solve problems, at least in the short term.

When I was eleven, my mother had a birthday present for me. I was excited. Presents were rare. My present? Mom got me a job. She walked me down to the newspaper branch and they gave me a newspaper route.

I delivered the *Chicago Tribune* seven days a week, every

week. I had one day off due to the flu, and once I took off two weeks to visit relatives in the Watts area of Los Angeles. Other than those two times, I delivered those papers seven days a week, every week from age 11 to age 16.

I would get up at 3:30 a.m. The driver from the branch, a man called Big George, would pick me up and we would head to the branch. I would finish my route, get home, bathe, and go to school.

Naturally, I had the biggest route in the branch.

The first time I ever suffered frostbite was delivering papers during those God-awful Chicago winters.

The branch manager would give us a candy bar at the start of our route. For energy, I guess. We would line up to get our candy.

One time I was in line and a boy named Kenny jumped in front of me. I grabbed his coat collar and swung him behind me with force, hitting his head on one of the wooden benches. His head split and blood flowed. Kenny wasn't hurt that badly, but as we know head wounds bleed profusely and he was in pain. The branch manager yelled at me. Kenny lay on the floor, trying to stop the bleeding and cussing.

I simply said, "You shouldn't have jumped in front of me."

I was twelve years old at the time.

None of the other 25 black youngbloods in the room said anything to me or tried to come to Kenny's aid. It was a non-event. Except in the eyes of the white branch manager. The white manager couldn't believe such a casual act of violence could occur so quickly. He was also probably worried about his liability. A group of young men under his supervision were engaged in violence that caused blood to flow. It happened on his watch.

Drunk Sam

We had hobos. Men who worked for money periodically but primarily they were free spirits that bothered no one. They were philosophers by nature, travelers of the world by choice.

They would ride the rails (jump freight trains) and move from city to city.

However, there were also winos. These men were of a different breed. Often, they were thieves, drunkards, very belligerent, and generally not to be trusted.

Our Evanston home sat on a dead-end street that backed up to the "Canal," an open body of water that carried liquid God-knows-what from one point to another. Along the Canal was a path interspersed with undergrowth, stubby trees, and bushes. In this area, a group of winos resided. One such wino was a man we called Drunk Sam.

One Saturday afternoon I was playing stickball in the street with my neighbor Cecil and his two sisters. We were 13 to 14 years old. There were four of us.

Drunk Sam approached our group and tried to sexually assault one of Cecil's sisters.

I grabbed Drunk Sam and spun him, and Cecil hit the man. A nice right cross to the jaw. Sam went down and fell in the street.

He was wearing an old, tattered suit coat with inside pockets. As he hit the ground the coat flew open. On the right side was a pint of cheap whiskey, but on the left side we could see the handle of a large butcher knife.

Sam said, "I am going to kill all you damn kids." He came up reaching for the knife.

Years later I thought about that event. The four of us didn't run away; we didn't yell, scream, or panic, nor did we call for help. We circled him. Our plan of action was simple. Whichever one he attacked with the butcher knife, the other three would attack him, putting him down once more.

Only this time he wasn't getting up so quickly. That was our mind set.

We never had the chance. My mother was watching from the window. She came roaring out of the house. As it so happened, on the ground alongside the fence to our home, lay an old-fashioned toy fire truck. It was large, bright red, heavy duty, and made of cast iron.

She picked up the cast-iron toy fire truck and began beating Sam across his head and shoulders. All the while Mom cussed a blue streak and yelled, "Leave those kids alone!"

Normally, if your mother is in a street fight with another man, you assist your mom. In this case, it became apparent if Mom kept at it, she was going to kill Sam.

I flashed back to when my grandmother stabbed Bailey, and he almost died. I remembered the description of the blood that had to be cleaned up, Bailey, who had to be stitched up and Grandma going to jail. It was a hassle.

Thus, I grabbed Mom to stop her from beating Sam to death.

He managed to stumble off, saying, "Lady, I don't want no trouble."

We let him go.

After that there was no more trouble from Drunk Sam or any of the other winos.

Danger

We lived with violence but our behavior, upon occasion, placed us in dangerous situations of a different sort.

The Third Rail

During my early teenage years, I would travel with older kids from the neighborhood, usually Saturday morning, via the L to the South Side of Chicago. Sometimes we were down there to simply hangout. At other times we were able to scrape together enough money to see a show at the Regal Theatre, 4719 South Parkway. The street is now called South Martin Luther King Drive.

The dollars needed for the theatre in variably left us short on already limited funds. Thus, on a routine basis we would "hop" the L.

We discovered a way to climb up an embankment, shimmy along a very narrow platform that ran along a wall, climb down from the platform, and walk along the tracks for a short distance. We then climbed up to the main platform and waited for the train. This action avoided buying a ticket.

One such time, my older running buddies were in front of me and had completed the process. They had reached the main platform.

I was the youngest, slowest but not necessarily the smallest. I found myself on the very narrow platform and before I could disembark and travel the short distance along the tracks, I heard a train coming.

The platform was so narrow I couldn't walk normally, I had part of my body hanging in space over the tracks. The space soon to be occupied by an oncoming train.

I remember distinctly pressing my body flat against the wall, turning my face from left to right, and then the train arrived. A train traveling at a very high rate of speed. The passenger cars passed only a few inches away from my face.

It was imperative that I remain absolutely still. Unfortunately, the passing train created a vacuum cleaner effect and began sucking me toward the speeding passengers' cars. This was my first memorable lesson in physics.

Fortunately, my weight allowed me to remain flat against the wall.

Finally, in what seemed an eternity the train, was gone.

I proceeded to climb down the narrow platform and walk along the tracks. At the last minute, I remembered not to step on the Third Rail. This was the electrified rail that powered the Chicago trains. The Third Rail contained 600 volts of electricity—more than enough to kill a man.

Given what I had just experienced, stepping on the Third Rail and electrocuting myself to death would have been a very catastrophic and silly way to start a Saturday morning.

One last point: As I climbed up on the main platform, my running buddies and other people on the main platform who had witnessed the entire event were all staring at me.
Although no one said a word.

Butch and a Wakeup Call

Mom had a cousin named Doris. Doris, dead now, was a good person. Butch, her son, not so much.

He had tremendous flaws, including being a thief, but the man could fight. Once while still relatively young, Butch fought a man older and bigger. He put the man on the ground and Butch laughed at the man, saying, "I thought you could fight."

This man's friend walked up behind Butch and shot him four times. Butch didn't die. He was a thick, muscular man, and the shooter was using a .22 caliber Roscoe. Before we could track down the shooter, said shooter was involved in another shooting. Only this time, he killed a man in public. The shooter went to prison behind that one.

Two things happened to Butch that were a wakeup call for him. Almost being shot to death was the first. The second, he met a good woman. He put his thuggish ways behind him, married her, and moved down south and started a family.

Years after starting his new life, he died. He died before his time. I believe the four bullet wounds shortened his life, but the remaining life he did have was a good one.

Chapter 5

Elementary School: Red Rock Prison

I ATTENDED AN ALL-BLACK SCHOOL NAMED FOSTER ELEMENTARY School, a large red brick building. The black people nicknamed the school the Red Rock Prison.

Mom also attended Foster Elementary School. Her generation also had called it the Red Rock Prison.

As a class of people, we were poor, angry, black, and prone to violent action to settle disputes. In grade school, I learned to fight in the streets. At Foster, a boy pulled a knife on me for the first time, which I handled.

At school, I learned to never back up or shy away from a confrontation. At Foster, the type of man I wanted to be began to form in my psyche.

Yes, we called it Red Rock Prison. In reality, the school predominately employed white teachers who did the very best they could.

I am no mental health care professional. However, I came to believe that having children (just starting out in life) nickname their elementary school as a prison was not a good thing.

A quick note regarding bullies. I don't understand how the young of today allow bullies to torment them.

In my day, if a weaker child was bullied, the weaker child

would simply wait. At some point the bully would turn his back. The weaker child would then hit the bully in the back of the head with half a brick. When he fell, the hitting would continue until the bully didn't move anymore.

Problem solved.

Junior High School

In the sixth grade I graduated from Foster Elementary School and attended one of the three junior high schools located in Evanston. All three schools (which covered our seventh and eighth grades) were in wealthy, white, upscale parts of Evanston. I had never seen so many white people in one place in my life. Out of 25 kids in my seventh-grade math class, perhaps five were black.

We were seriously intimidated. Often, I would know the answer to the teacher's question, but I wouldn't raise my hand.

However, it wasn't long before I discovered I wasn't the smartest kid in school, but I was one of the smartest. I wasn't the strongest or best athlete, but I was one of the strongest and best athletically.

I gained confidence and continued along the journey of determining what type of man I wanted to become.

I had a teacher talk me into entering a poetry contest. As part of the competition, I had to recite the poem in front of the entire seventh and eighth grade classes in the school auditorium. It was the "Song of Summer" by Paul Lawrence Dunbar.

I was one of the winners, and I was 14 years old. I discovered I was good in sports but could also speak in front of people easily.

One other thing I discovered: If white people were new to us, we were new to them.

I had a science teacher in eighth grade. Apparently, he was a navigator on a bomber during World War II and a very aggressive man.

The war never left him.

He had a system of keeping order in the classroom. He absolutely didn't allow students to speak out of turn in his class. He had a long hard wooden pointer used to point at information on the blackboard. He had modified this pointer by adding a bell.

If a student was talking out of turn during class, he would ring the bell. If the student kept talking, he would strike the student across the back or shoulders with this stout wooden cane.

As luck would have it, I was standing next to a boy who was talking. The teacher thought I was the one talking, and he struck me across my shoulder with this cane.

I wheeled on him and punched right in his nose. Down he went. I was only 14 but strong and could punch (all those mornings pushing a heavy cart of newspapers).

Believe me, the classroom went silent. Keep in mind this was the time in our nation's history when a student hit a teacher, the student was expelled; he was headed for reform school etc. To make matters worse, I struck a white man in public. I felt I was in for a world of hurt.

He picked himself up off the floor, his nose bleeding profusely. I vividly remember him taking tissues from a box of Kleenex on his desk and sticking the tissues up his nose to absorb the blood.

He looked at me and calmly said, "John, you can go back to your desk now."

That was it. I never got in trouble with the authorities.

As I said earlier, white people were new to us, but black kids must have been new to some of these white teachers.

What exactly did he think was going to happen when he hit a young black man with a cane?

An odd thing occurred. For the rest of the semester no student ever spoke out of turn and the teacher never struck another student.

Humor (with a twist)

Our lives weren't filled with constant fighting and dangerous situations.

We found humor as well.

Mom once told me as a young girl she would often get into fights. On one such occasion there was a girl who wanted to do battle. As luck would have it, Mom was wearing a "new" dress. She went home, changed into some old clothes, then returned to the scene and fought this girl, whose "ass she whipped."

Mom told me with pride that with all her fights, her older brother (Monroe) never needed to "take up for me." In other words, Monroe never assisted her in a fist fight.

However, Mom did say once that she needed Monroe's help. It was the one fight where she was stabbed with an ice pick, which wasn't fair. Monroe jumped in to even the score. That was the only time he assisted her in a battle.

When Mom was telling this story her mother, Grandmother Viola said, "The stab wound couldn't have been that bad. You are still here aren't you?"

They laughed (this is the humor with a twist). Mom wasn't murdered in an ice pick attack so why complain about the attack being unfair?

I laughed with them. However, even though I was only in my early teens, I knew this really wasn't funny.

More Humor

I carried a knife throughout school. Jesse's weapon of choice was an ice pick. (What's with these ice picks?)

Jesse, Mom, and I belonged to the Mount Zion Missionary Baptist Church. Jesse and Mom sang in the choir. Then, as now, black men were incarcerated at a much higher rate than we are as a percentage of the U.S. population.

As part of Mount Zion's missionary outreach, the choir traveled by bus to visit prisons in Illinois. They sang gospel hymns to the prisoners and served them a home-cooked meal.

I have visited friends in prison, and it is a very depressing experience. Even visitors are thoroughly searched, as was the case with Jesse.

Jesse tried to enter the prison carrying a concealed weapon, his ice pick. Believe me, all hell broke loose.

They wouldn't let Jesse enter the prison and confined him to the bus. Jesse was one of the main cooks for the meal that was to be served. He also had several solo hymns to sing.

He couldn't participate. In fact, Mom had to bring him his supper, which he ate on the bus. She was very, very angry with him.

The prison officials tried explaining to him that prisons were a dangerous place. A place where ice picks weren't allowed. Jesse said he agreed. Prisons were a dangerous place which is why he NEEDED his ice pick.

Years later, we laughed about this situation. Once again, even though I laughed with everyone else, the situation wasn't particularly funny to me. Instead of surrendering his ice pick, Jesse chose to miss this important missionary event. I always wondered about his decision.

CHAPTER 6

Stepbrother

JESSE HAD A SON, MICHAEL, WHICH MEANT I HAD A STEPBROTHER during my teen years. Michael and I were never close. He spent most of his young adult and adult years in prison. Once I spoke to his parole officer, who said there were people who made a mistake, went to prison, learned their lesson, and became good citizens. My stepbrother wasn't one of them.

The parole officer said my brother Michael was a career criminal. He was one of those souls who was more comfortable in prison than out in the world.

To say my stepbrother was into crime is a statement that is too simple. He was into short cuts that led to crime that led to prison.

Michael, although younger than I, is now dead. His lifestyle, combined with his diabetes, was not conducive to a long life.

All he ever brought Jesse and my mother was pain.

Although my stepbrother did have one redeeming quality: his widow and his three children are very fine people.

Epileptic fits

During my early teen years, Mom would have epileptic fits upon occasion. Triggered by stress, perhaps, but for a long time no one truly seemed to know for sure what would bring on the seizures.

This occurred during the time when Big Momma lived with my stepbrother, Mom, Jesse, and me.

When Mom had her screaming, thrashing, pure manic violent explosions, I was the only one to assist.

In fact, the other three would stand as far away as possible and watch me. They offered no assistance. They were terrified.

I would hold Mom down while she screamed and thrashed. Mom was 5'4" and weighed 120 pounds. Despite her small size, it took everything I had to physically restrain her (without causing injury).

A teacher at school explained to me how to hold Mom's tongue down with my thumb during her fits. This prevented her from swallowing her tongue and choking to death.

What the teacher failed to tell me was Mom would bite my thumb with such force I thought I was going to lose the digit.

I was fourteen when this craziness began.

Fortunately, Northwestern University had an excellent health care plan for its employees. The doctors finally discovered Mom had a growth on her brain. Unfortunately, the mass was so intertwined in the core of the brain that surgery was impossible.

The doctors used medication to shrink the mass to a manageable level. For years afterward, Mom would say, "Johnny, my head is worrying me."

I would say, "Did you take your medication?"

Once I reminded her, she would take the medication and would be fine.

Again, I say thank you, Northwestern University, for the health insurance you provided Jesse.

Psychological Pain

The instances where my family has endured racism are too numerous to count. I will only relate the following story.

My grandmother and her crew of three ladies were going to serve a dinner party for a prominent white family in Highland Park, Illinois. This is a very, very upscale enclave of predominately Jewish citizens located 25 miles north of Downtown Chicago.

Grandma and her ladies were well groomed in their persons and immaculately dressed in their black-and-white uniforms.

As they pulled up to the mansion of a house, three young white girls roughly 12 years in age were playing outside. These young girls saw Grandma and her ladies arrive. The girls began screaming, "Run for your lives. Run for your lives, the niggers are coming!"

And they ran, terrified, into the house in question as the lady of the house opened the front door. The lady of the house was mightily embarrassed; she apologized profusely on and on.

1. However, the lady of the house never made the young girls apologize.
2. The lady of the house was afraid herself. She was afraid Grandma and her crew would walk off the job and not serve this dinner party.
3. Those little girls weren't born with that irrational fear and the "N" word planted in their brains. Somebody had taught them.
4. The little girls were truly afraid.

I could continue making additional points, but you get the idea.

We never know when we are going to be subjected to a difficult (at times life threatening) situation simply because we are black.

By the way, Grandma and her crew did serve the dinner party. Grandma simply charged the lady of the house twice their normal fee. The white woman was only too happy to pay.

CHAPTER 7

How We Arrived in the North and Our Relationship with Whites

ACCORDING TO THE NATIONAL ARCHIVES, "THE GREAT MIGRA-tion" refers to the large-scale movement of African Americans from the South to Northern cities such as Chicago. We wanted to escape the Jim Crow laws of the South. There were also manu-facturing jobs in the North.

This is what pulled my family to the Chicago area in the early 1900s. Chicago in general and Evanston in particular.

When exactly did my family arrive in Evanston is lost in time. However, the Jim Crow laws of the South was a driving force in our location from South Carolina We moved North and found jobs catering to the white elite of Evanston and Chicago's North Shore.

The relationship we had with whites was complicated. My mother had multiple jobs but she got to the point where her pri-mary place of employment was for a Mr. and Mrs. Eppstein. The Eppstein's had three children. Children that were privileged and of the elite. Mom would cook, clean, iron the family's clothes. There were times I would travel with mom to the Eppsteins if there was a chore that involved moving heavy furniture or the like.

We were their servants in every sense of the word, and yet when their children misbehaved, which was often, and the children would not mind their parents, my mother was called upon to correct the situation. The children obeyed my mother and did what she said the first time she said it. Mom would not tolerate bad behavior from me or them. Mom would say, "I will make you straighten up and fly right."

In time, the three children became adults and had children of their own. The exact same thing happened. My mother, in effect, raised the Eppstein's children's children. Mom raised the children and grandchildren.

There was another aspect to the relationship. I remember at one point in time our church Mount Zion Missionary Baptist Church needed a new roof. As a poor black church, we were struggling to raise all the funds needed for the roof replacement.

One Sunday Mr. and Mrs. Eppstein attended our church service, which they had never done before. Afterward they asked me to introduce them to the church Treasurer which I did.

They gave the Treasurer a check for several thousand dollars. The money needed to complete the new roof project.

I am sure they wrote off the donation on their taxes, but no one forced them to make this donation. My mother, the congregation and I were stunned.

One final point on this topic. At the end of her life Mrs. Eppstein had cancer. Mom said Mrs. Eppstein only wanted my mother to care for her. Not her husband, not her children, not her friends. Only my mother. Mom said she would bathe Mrs. Eppstein, and that cancer had whittled her down to almost nothing. Mom told me it was like lifting a small child out of the bathtub.

As stated, our relationship with white people was at times complicated.

The Veil

Monroe Williams, my uncle, my mother's brother, was the first-born child of Viola, my grandmother.

I remember Uncle Monroe as a person who was always kind to me. For example, he was the one who taught me directions. He taught me North was always on the left side of East and because we lived not far from Lake Michigan the sun always rose over Lake Michigan to the East.

He was a big man who was a Specialist 5 in the US Army and saw some of the worst fighting in World War II. Uncle Monroe explained how there would be a lull in the fighting, in a given battle. The men would stop to eat their rations. However, first Uncle Monroe said he would flick the brains from his uniform. The brains of a fellow soldier that had been killed in the recent fight. Uncle Monroe would explain this to me in a very matter-of-fact manner. I was a preteen, and it was during the time frame my sire had abandoned us and before Mom was re-married to Jesse.

I had few adult males in my life and Uncle Monroe took an interest in me.

It was well known in our family that Uncle Monroe was born with a veil over his face.

According to Very Well Health (verywellhealth.com): When a baby is born with a veil over its face, it's called a *caul birth*, or an *en caul birth*.

This rare occurrence happens when a small piece of the amniotic sac covers the baby's face or head, giving it the appearance of being in a bubble. An *en caul* birth is similar to a standard birth in that the doctor will carefully snip the sac and allow the fluid to leak out.

However, some people believe that being born *en caul* has a spiritual significance and that the child is protected. For example, sailors once believed that the caul was a protective talisman that protected them from drowning.

Uncle Monroe Left Us

Evanston Review, 1963

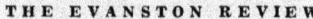

THE EVANSTON REVIEW

ing in the Hebblethwaite chapel was followed by a requiem mass in St. Nicholas Church.

Burial was in Mt. Carmel Cemetery, Hillside.

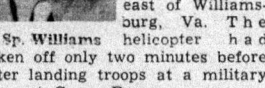

SPECIALIST 5 WASHINGTON M. WILLIAMS, 39, son of Mrs. Viola Bailey, 1241 Emerson street, was injured fatally in a crash of an army helicopter Apr. 19. Specialist Williams and two others were killed in the crash in a wooded area in James City County, nine miles east of Williamsburg, Va. The helicopter had taken off only two minutes before after landing troops at a military base at Camp Peary.

Specialist Williams, who was educated in Evanston's elementary schools and graduated from Evanston High School, was a veteran of World War II overseas service in Germany. After his discharge from service, he returned here and then enrolled in a college in Little Rock, Ark.

After his marriage, he reenlisted in the army in 1955.

Surviving, besides his mother and wife, Elizabeth, of Hyattsville, Md., are two sons, Thaddeus, 11, and Marcus, 6; a daughter, Franzetta, 13, and three sisters, Mrs. Jannie Bowman and Mrs. Etta Hillard, both of Los Angeles, and Mrs. Bertha Minor, 2019 Grey avenue.

A military service was conducted Apr. 24 in Washington, D.C., with burial in Arlington Cemetery.

Specialist 5 Washington Monroe Williams, 39, son of Mrs. Viola Bailey was injured fatally in a crash of an army helicopter April 19, 1963. Specialist Williams and two others were killed in the crash in a wooded area in James City County nine miles east of Williamsburg VA.

He was a veteran of World War II overseas service in Germany. After his discharge from service, he married and reenlisted in the army in 1955.

Military service was conducted April 24, 1963, in Washington DC, with burial in Arlington Cemetery.

He was 39 years old at the time of his death. My uncle survived some of the worst fighting in Germany during WWII, only to be killed in a helicopter crash during peace time.

I know the family kept a lock of his childhood hair and his veil. The hair remained but the veil was lost.

Did the veil he was born under keep him safe during the war and then, after the war, it didn't because the veil was lost?

I will never know. I do know this. Because of my Uncle Monroe I know after death there is the "other side."

Why?

In 1963, I was only 14 years old. Despite this fact my family gave me the task of telling Big Momma, my great grandmother, that her grandson, Uncle Monroe had been killed.

I knocked on Big Momma's door and she said enter. I walked in and without preamble told her Uncle Monroe had been killed the previous evening.

She had a sad, calm look on her face and told me, "I know. Last night he came to me and said goodbye."

My uncle spoke to his grandmother from the "other side."

CHAPTER 8

Careless Acts of Kindness

OVER THE YEARS I HAVE DISPLAYED CARELESS ACTS OF KINDNESS.

The Main and Grant

In the summers, since there was no school, I would often work two jobs. A day job coupled with my early morning paper route.

It was the summer of my 16th year. I had completed my shift, my day job, as a bus boy at the Orrington Hotel in downtown Evanston. A very upscale facility. I walked several blocks to catch the bus home since it was very important that I arrived home in time to complete my chores and then off to bed. Big George from the Paper Route Branch would be at my home at 3:30 a.m. to pick me up and transport me to the branch. My morning *Chicago Tribune* paper route began shortly after my arrival at the branch.

I arrived at the bus stop and the following unfolded: A taxicab pulled up at the bus stop and a white lady, in her middle years got out of the cab. She was well dressed and professional in her appearance. The cab driver drove away. This woman with two suitcases stood there, perplexed and confused.

There were several of us standing at the bus stop and as it so happens, we were all black. Catching the same bus to our part of town.

The lady said to no one in particular, "I am looking for the Orrington Hotel."

No one said a word, even though we knew full well where the hotel was located.

Why did the cab driver drop her off at a location, obviously several city blocks from the hotel, with two pieces of luggage, luggage that appeared to be heavy, on a warm summer day?

I don't know. The fact no one was willing to at least point her in the right direction was also something I didn't understand then or now.

I looked up and the bus was arriving, the Main and Grant bus, my bus. I looked at the bus and then at this out of her depth woman and I began to quietly curse under my breath.

The next bus wasn't for an hour or more, and I needed to get home. I had a routine that worked but a fairly tight schedule had to be maintained.

In frustration at the situation and with myself, I walked over to the woman, grabbed a bag in each hand—the bags weren't light—and said, "Follow me." I never introduced myself, never asked her where she was from or her name. I simply headed several blocks back to my place of summer employment where I had been earlier in the day.

This lady struggled to keep up with my angry strides. She was wearing high heels. The kind that makes a woman's bottom wiggle when she walks fast. We called them "CFM" shoes: "Come Fuck Me" shoes.

I wasn't angry with her, only with my stupid do-good attitude.

We arrived at the hotel in good order, and she gave me a $2.00

tip. If possible, I would have paid $2.00 not to miss my bus and alter my schedule.

I say a random act of kindness. Yes, I was upset that my schedule was altered, but other than a relatively short delay, I wasn't harmed.

The Wild Man

I was in my early forties and owned a big black Lincoln Continental. I was returning from a meeting on a Saturday afternoon in downtown Milwaukee. It was a hot summer day. In fact, it was very hot as in 95-degree heat with a heat index which pushed the temperature even higher. I was heading north on a city street with few trees, a cloudless sky and blazing sun.

As I passed a bus stop, I noticed a public bus cruising down the street with an agitated man, an agitated black man, chasing the bus, obviously attempting to have the bus driver stop. The bus driver was oblivious and kept driving. The man was beyond angry, shouting and cursing as he approached a woman, who I assumed to be his wife, and an infant in a stroller. They were waiting at the bus stop for his return. No other passengers were at this stop, only the three of them.

It was hot, no shade and a very stressful situation for them.

I passed them by in no time. My knowledge of weekend bus schedules was nonexistent, but even if they had to wait a short while in that heat it would not have been good.

As I continued driving, my mind was working. I'm thinking I don't know this man, but I know his type. To say he could be unpredictable was an understatement. I don't normally talk to myself but, in this instance, I said out loud. "John T, this could be a very bad decision. This was a mistake waiting to happen."

Because I was thinking about offering them a ride. Understand my reasoning—the man in question wasn't overly big, but he was wild in his dress, long hair all over the place, agitated in his movement and bearing. The missed bus aside, here was a man constantly mad at the world and everything in it.

Circling the block, I pulled up next to where they were standing. Rolling down the window, I addressed the man saying, "I noticed the bus passed you by. It's hot out. Can I give you and your family a ride home?"

He stared at me and stared at me not saying a word. His wife was mute; even the baby was quiet. I simply kept my vision on him, not repeating myself. It had to be more than 30 seconds that we locked eyes, then he nodded once.

Popping the trunk, I said, "Place the stroller inside, get in the car, and I will take you home."

The woman got into the back and buckled herself in and buckled the infant in the seat next to her.

He sat next to me. He gave me directions when asked. The location was one of the worst neighborhoods imaginable. This hood would have given the South Side of Chicago a run for its money.

It wasn't simply the rundown homes, unkept yards, and feeling of danger, but there was an air of hopelessness and sense of sadness.

The hood was in despair.

As we drove, he suddenly expressed his anger at the bus driver. My passenger said, "I am not a violent man, but if I ever catch that bus driver . . ." His voice trailed off. I glanced at him and there was a touch of insanity in his eyes.

We arrived at their destination, as they exited the car the

woman quietly said, "Thank you." Her man never did thank me. He never asked my name or anything about me. He simply left the vehicle.

There was one final thing of note. As he removed the stroller from the trunk, I glanced in the rear-view mirror. He slammed the trunk down, looked me in the eyes, slapped both hands together, hard, and pushed his hands toward me.

I believe it was his way of saying thanks, but he was also telling me, yes you know where we live but I don't ever want to see you again.

I say this was a careless act of kindness because when I stopped, I wasn't in a hurry to get to my destination.

If it hadn't been for that child, I never would have assisted this family.

The child made the difference, but only just.

I say these examples were careless acts of kindness. In both cases I had to alter my path to accommodate other people. I suffered no real hardship. Yes, I had to wait for the next Main and Grant bus to arrive, and yes, I spent a little time taking that family home. However, I didn't suffer any significant pain by offering assistance.

My actions could be described as neither here nor there. I simply treated those people as one human should treat another.

CHAPTER 9

Maxwell Street

The City of Chicago website describes Maxwell Street as follows: Maxwell Street first appeared on a Chicago map in 1847. The street was named after Philip Maxwell (1799–1859), an Army surgeon who went on to become the state Treasurer of Illinois.

In an era of civil unrest and political change, Maxwell Street Market, founded by the Jewish community, thrived as a multi-cultural phenomenon and was even called the "Ellis Island of the Midwest."

In my early years, we would periodically hop the L and travel to the West Side and visit Maxwell Street. It was exciting and perhaps potentially a bit dangerous. We were on the West Side of Chicago, not our part of town, but Maxwell Street catered to all types of people.

I mention Maxwell Street for the following reason. My visits to Maxwell Street at an early age helped me realize that people from different backgrounds can co-exist. Conflict between different groups of people is not always a given.

Chicago

I have always found Chicagoland complex. Growing up, we all understood Chicago was a rigged town. It was hardwired into the city's DNA for various reasons. One reason was Al Capone.

Chicago was Al Capone's home. He was the head of a crime organization called The Outfit. That was what they called themselves. Not the Mafia, the Outfit.

Did Capone's influence help make Chicago irreverent when it comes to law? Or did the lawless environment of Chicago allow Capone to prosper?

I don't know. As I said, Chicago is complicated.

I do know this: In my travels across America and other countries, I have never heard anyone say people from Chicago are weak. Particularly if you are black.

If you are black and from Chicagoland, you have a certain level of toughness.

Otherwise, you wouldn't be here.

The Chicago influence helped mold me into the man I am today.

CHAPTER 10

Evanston Township High School (ETHS)

I entered high school in 1964. ETHS was one of the top-rated public schools in the nation. Students from all races and economic backgrounds attended the school.

The school had 5,000 students. That's right, 5,000. There were over 350 students in my homeroom, which resembled a bowling alley in size. By the time I was a senior and graduated, there were over 1,000 students in my graduating class.

We were a city within a city. As in keeping with most cities, there were a kaleidoscope of forces at work both psychological and physical.

I have heard tales about how hard and difficult high school was for certain people. It was difficult to fit in or be with the cool kids. It wasn't hard for me. At least not in that sense.

My freshman year I did what everyone else I grew up with was doing. Running the streets, shooting dice, drinking cheap wine, fighting men, and chasing women. It's what we did.

Often after running the streets with my fellow paper route friends at 1:00 a.m. on a Saturday night we would head home saying, "See you in a few hours."

Around 3:30 a.m., the drivers from the paper route branch

would pick us up at our home because it was time to deliver the *Chicago Tribune*, Sunday edition.

There were times still early on Sunday morning I would arrive home very tired after completing my paper route. I would say to Mom and Big Momma, "I am too tired to attend church."

Big Momma would say, "If you can cabaret Saturday night, you can go to church Sunday morning."

I went to church.

My Wake-Up Moment

Late in my freshman year in high school, a janitor (who was a gracious black gentleman) said he wanted to speak to me. He told me his job as a janitor wasn't a bad job, but he didn't want to see me doing it. I was better than that.

Shortly thereafter another gracious man of color pointed out a young man who had graduated from ETHS and gone on to college only to blow it.

This young man was an excellent athlete. He was back in Evanston doing some things but basically doing nothing. Given his talent, the gentlemen speaking to me felt this young man was a waste.

It was then I decided I was going to college, and I was going to make it work.

This was my Wake-Up moment, my Epiphany.

Prior to this time my studies were a thing I did in passing. Beginning my sophomore year, I really buckled down and began to work hard, not only to improve my grades but to learn.

I also started to participate in sports in earnest. I played football in the fall, wrestled in the winter, and played lacrosse in the spring.

I participated in all these sports and by my senior year was an excellent wrestler and named an All-State Offensive Guard in Football for the state of Illinois.

I drank only in the off-season, cut back on running the streets, and reduced my womanizing.

Another fact was brought home to me. Once my teachers saw I was attempting to turn my life around they bent over backward to assist.

They would stay late if I had a problem I was struggling to solve, gave me extra homework when I requested it, and encouraged me to speak out in class when I knew the answer to the questions asked.

To this day my respect for teachers has no limits.

Due to my change in attitude, my high school challenges were slightly different. I had black "friends" who would attack white people simply because they were white. This was a stupid idea in my opinion.

Also, I was approached by other "friends" who said Doctor Martin Luther King Jr. would be in Chicago leading a peace march. I was asked to partake in the march. However, I was told no matter what the white people said or did we couldn't fight back. It would be a peaceful, non-violent march.

I also thought this was a stupid idea. You can't include me in that non-violence nonsense while I am being attacked.

I had multiple teammates due to my sports activities. However, I had very, very few friends. I went my own way in high school, which at times was a struggle.

Savannah

Going my own way caused several people not to like me. A black female student named Savannah was one of them. She felt I had too many white friends. That wasn't the case. I simply saw no reason to attack someone simply because they were white.

Savannah was a strong, handsome, robust young woman, with three very tough brothers. Think of Serena Williams with a very bad attitude.

That was Savannah.

I have always loved to read. Back in those days there was a News Stand just off Howard Street that I would visit.

Howard Street was the northern dividing line between Evanston and Chicago's North Side. People speak of how tough the South Side of Chicago was (and is) which is true. The same can be said for the West and North sides of Chicago. All of Chicago was and is tough.

Late one evening in early winter, I was walking toward the newsstand. I was 16 at the time and was wearing a brand new overcoat. A coat purchased using earnings from my paper route.

This was a coat I desperately needed with winter approaching.

In front of me was an elderly white woman also heading toward the newsstand. I'm thinking this lady doesn't belong in this neighborhood as night is falling. She is asking for trouble, which is exactly what she received.

Two black young bloods about my age swooped out of nowhere pushed her hard and grabbed the purse she had hung over her left shoulder and took off running.

They hit this woman hard but for some reason she was able to keep her feet and not fall. She began screaming.

I threw off my coat which landed on the ground. It is much better to run (and fight) without a heavy winter coat impeding your movements.

These two thieves did exactly what they were supposed to do as they ran away. They split up with one taking a right-hand turn while the other (the one with the purse) continued running straight.

I followed the one with the purse. All the while yelling "Drop the purse. I don't want you I only want the purse."

He kept running and he could fly. Although in those days I was fast myself.

Now the danger in this situation is the one thief who split to the right circles back and is now behind me. Would he have a gun? Probably not. Would he have a knife? Probably so.

Thus, I am running, watching the hands of the thief I am chasing, looking for a gun or knife. At the same time, I am listening for footsteps from behind me.

Footsteps that would belong to the second thief who would want to cover for his partner in crime by stabbing me in the back.

The thief I am chasing turns into an alley that dead-ends into a moderately high fence. He stops to open the purse, remove the cash and flee. He can't get the purse open quickly. I am bearing down on him, still shouting, "Drop the purse!"

This he finally does. He drops the purse without having been able to open it and scampers over the fence. I immediately turned to make sure his buddy wasn't behind me.

I take the purse to the lady who is still on the sidewalk sobbing. Upon seeing me she is thankful, thankful, thankful. I said, "If you want to thank me, stay out of this neighborhood at night."

My emotions at the time were pure anger, not at the thieves, nor the woman, but at myself. I could have been stabbed. For what? An attempt to retrieve a purse that held a few dollars for a woman who was a total stranger. A woman who should have known better than to be in that area. However, my real anger and regret was knowing my brand-new coat would be gone. My coat lying on the ground would disappear. It would have been stolen by someone.

I walked a few steps and looked up and there was Savannah. I had never seen her in that part of town before. She said to me in a nasty tone of voice, "Well, aren't you the hero."

Savannah was holding my coat!

She gave me the coat and I said thank you. She said you are welcome and walked away.

I don't have the words to describe what Savannah did:

1. She didn't like me at all and actually despised white people.
2. I am certain she had better things to do than wait in failing light in that neighborhood for me to return and retrieve my coat.
3. She took a position; she took ownership and responsibility for that coat. **There was no force on the face of this earth that would have been able to take that coat from Savannah.** This woman could fight. However, you never knew when some mad man might have tried to steal the coat. She was willing to place herself at risk for me.

I will always wonder why she helped me.

For the rest of our time in high school we never became friends. However, the intense animosity between us was gone.

Violence During My High School Years

Charles Ballard could fight. His fists were fast, and he packed a punch. He had a fight with Junior Jones. Charles beat Junior soundly. When Junior recovered, he caught up with Charles.

Junior had four of his friends hold Charles while Junior stabbed Charles to death in the street late one night.

Travis beat Matt one on one in a basketball game. Matt was offended. He then stabbed Travis to death on the playground adjacent to Red Rock Prison.

Marsha Willis had a brother named David. A big cocky outlaw of a man. David cheated a group of Chicago drug dealers. The drug dealers cut off his head. The authorities found the torso but never the head.

In all of those cases the police—"the man"—didn't particularly care. It was violence done by black people upon black people. Junior and Matt did a little time, and the murderers of David were never apprehended.

Violence Lessons Learned

I learned specific concepts from my people, but I also learned general concepts from violence.

1. **Always carry a knife.** Note: To this day I don't carry but still have the gravity/switch blade I carried back in the day.
2. Generally speaking, as long as black people were killing black people the cops and courts didn't care.
3. Never piss off Chicago drug dealers.

Side Note: Kim was a girl in high school that I really liked. For the longest time she had no interest in me. Then one day she changed. We began to date, and I was a happy young man.

Then Kim gave me my first Dear John letter. She was Charles Ballard's girlfriend, but he dumped her for another girl. Kim in her letter admitted she only began dating me to make Charles jealous. She hoped he would take her back. It worked; he wanted her back to which she agreed and then sent me the letter. I was sick with heartache.

Shortly thereafter Junior murdered Charles. As luck would have it, I passed Kim on the street the very next day. Tears were streaming down her face. I looked at her and said nothing.

4. The other lesson I learned from violence is that it can be a catalyst for karma.

CHAPTER 11

Death Is Capricious

DURING THESE EARLY YEARS IN HIGH SCHOOL, I CAME TO BELIEVE death was arbitrary, unpredictable, and capricious.

In addition to the deaths mentioned earlier in this writing, Papa Johnson had a son that was a professional baseball prospect with the Chicago Cubs. Before his son could sign, Papa's son was murdered in a drive by shooting. He wasn't even the target.

Tommy Langston died after accidently ingesting lead paint. How is that even possible? The answer was our homes were so aged that lead paint and asbestos were common.

Bill Boss, a fine young man and excellent at playing football stopped to assist a stranded motorist. A car hit Bill, killing him our senior year in high school.

Two blocks over a man came home and found his wife in bed with another woman. He pulled a gun and murdered them both.

He was on the loose for several days. Maybe because it was a double murder or maybe it was due to the sexual angle; in any case these murders hit the news cycle.

Therefore, the police pretended they cared. They warned us to be vigilant until the shooter could be apprehended.

We weren't concerned. The shooter wasn't going to pursue

anyone else. He had a specific incident that set him off and he did murder.

Even though I was only a teenager I felt he shouldn't have killed those women. If you catch your wife with another woman *in flagrante delicto*, the husband should either forgive his wife, divorce his wife, or tell his wife to move over please.

Who can explain death? Perhaps the people in my neighborhood and I were focusing on the quote from the Roman Emperor Marcus Aurelius (121-180 AD) "Death smiles at us all, all a man can do is smile back."

So why try to explain death? Or why go out of your way to avoid it. I have no answer to these question. I can only repeat one of my Big Momma's sayings. "Don't worry about the mule going blind just sit there and shake the line."

Don't worry about life and death; simply live your life.

Sex

While in junior high, most of us became sexually active. By high school, sex was old hat. It was something we did. It amused us to listen to the white students attempting to determine who was sexually active in their circle of friends.

Our big news would have been those black kids who weren't sexually active. It was no big deal. However, there were times it got out of hand.

When I was sixteen and a sophomore in high school, I had a sexual relationship with one of the high school teachers. She wasn't my teacher directly, but she was one of our high school teachers.

The affair was brief, intense, and sweet.

I told no one. Even then I knew a man shouldn't kiss and tell.

However, the authorities got wind of the affair from some other source. Maybe she told someone, who told someone else. I never found out for sure.

What did happen was the authorities tried hard to get me to confirm the relationship.

They used a three-pronged approach.

One, they appealed to my civic duty. Earlier in the year a white girl had lost her wallet, which was filled with money. Through dumb luck I found it and turned it into the office. She was in the office when I brought in the wallet. This girl was stunned when she discovered the cash was still in the wallet. I was thanked profusely by this young lady and the office personnel. They told me I was a fine young man. My thoughts were no that isn't the case. I am simply not a thief.

My interrogators used this example telling me I obviously cared about my fellow students. In keeping with this caring spirit, I should admit the sexual liaison took place. In this way I could protect other underage fragile students from this female predator.

They seemed to forget this was Chicagoland and people didn't rat out other people.

I looked them dead in the eye and lied. I said it never happened.

Now, Assistant Vice Principals and the Police have built in bullshit detectors hardwired into their psyche. They knew I was lying.

Thus, they tried approach number **Two.** They said we see you are turning your life around in terms of studying and sports participation. You are truly college-bound. What a fine young man you have become, blah, blah.

They were truly pumping sunshine up my shirt.

Still, I lied and said nothing happened.

Then they tried approach number **Three**, the stick. Son, if you don't tell the truth, it will be very difficult for your teachers to write letters of recommendation to ease your way into college. The powers that be will know you will have failed in your civic duty to yourself and your fellow students.

Now I am pissed off. They really were attacking the wrong person.

I told them again nothing happened.

Then they asked if I would consent to a polygraph. Without hesitation I said yes. I knew I could beat a lie detector test. Just remain calm and ice cold inside, which was my normal state of being when under duress. They never did give me that test.

Three grown men, all white, with authority over my future, had me in a room. I am a 16-year-old kid, no legal representation, no advocate to support me and no parents in attendance.

Only me.

They wanted me to believe this 25-year-old white girl of a woman had abused me. These three overbearing men, threaten my ability to attend college, they were the true abusers.

I smiled, lied, and maintained the inner ice. However, in my heart, I said, "FUCK the three of you forever."

I did find it odd that these three white men deemed it advisable not to include my football, wrestling, or lacrosse coaches in the discussion. Was it because my coaches would have given me a level of support and comfort these three men didn't want me to have?

My coaches might have also told these three men they were wasting their time.

Eventually, they let me go. In short order they did fire this teacher and later it came to my attention her career was ruined. Even without hard evidence they were able to remove this woman from her position.

Obviously, this woman had a problem, but it shouldn't have cost her the career of her choice.

She simply made a mistake.

It was just as obvious someone needed to be the adult in that bedroom. In this case it should have been me.

Ideally, I never should have gone into her bedroom in the first place.

I felt responsible for her predicament.

Decades later I was discussing this event with a close friend. As men age, they tend to discuss things that have caused them regret in their lives.

He had a similar story. My friend stated in years past he had sex with a nun. I was stunned. My transgression cost a woman her livelihood, reputation and standing in the community. My friend's outrageous behavior destroyed a woman's position in the church and jeopardized her well-being in numerous other ways.

His sin was much worse than mine. At least that was my initial opinion. However, upon reflection I decided we both were very wrong. We both may be destined for the very center of Dante's ninth circle of Hell, that special place in hell reserved for those who have betrayed a trust.

Time will tell.

Bootstraps

It was during high school that I first heard various white people state that they had worked hard and made a success of their lives on their own. It was the opinion of these whites that black people should do the same. "Pull yourself up by your own bootstraps."

At times they would use me as an example of how someone, who was black, underprivileged but turned their life around for good on their own.

I would respond yes, it is possible. Then I would relate the following story. On our block there was a young man named Joseph.

Joseph's mother was a junkie. She was hooked on crack as was the unfortunate plight of many black people. In fact, she was on crack when she became pregnant with Joseph.

Joseph was born a crack baby, addicted to crack cocaine day one out of the womb.

He never knew his father and his junkie mother died of an overdose. She drowned in her own bathtub.

Joseph was raised by his grandmother. He was 12 years old before he realized this woman wasn't his mother but his grandmother.

Joseph was a black boy born in racist America, hooked on crack in the womb, lived in a poor neighborhood, father completely out of the picture with a dead junkie mother. He is raised by his elderly grandmother who is fighting her own battles connected with an aging black woman.

I would say to these white people how is he supposed to make something of himself on his own?

Invariably the people to whom I was speaking became quiet. They didn't have a clue.

Now in reality with the help of the neighborhood and other outside forces Joseph did turn out alright. He got clean, graduated high school, went into the military and has made a good life for himself. However, he didn't break free without significant assistance.

There was no "Pull yourself up by your own bootstraps."

Cops and Being Black in America

At present the black Lives Matter concept is sweeping the country, as it should be.

So, what took so long?

Obviously, as a society we need the police. However, the police should never assault, harass, kill someone simply because they are black or brown.

I shall only relate one of my unpleasant encounters with the law.

It was during wrestling season in my junior year in highschool. The following Saturday was a bye week, which meant we had no wrestling matches for that coming Saturday.

The week after the bye Saturday we would be wrestling the Niles, Illinois team. We decided on our off Saturday, the bye week, to drive to Niles and watch that team wrestle since we would be in a contest with them in a few days.

There were four of us all black males aged 17 years old.

Upon leaving the Niles wrestling match, in the evening, the Niles East Police pulled us over. They demanded we follow them to their police station.

There they placed the four us in an interview room with multiple white police officers. The cops began to grill us. Why were we in that neighborhood at night, what were we up to, who were we going to see? All in authoritarian, nasty, aggressive tone of voice.

My three friends were terrified, but I was pissed off. I did my best to maintain my composure.

Sadly, I failed.

I told the lead big cop. Who had a huge belly. "We told you who we are, you checked our respective driver's licenses verifying our identities. You tore our car apart looking for drugs, weapons (it was one of the few times we left our knives at home on purpose) and found none. Further, there are no warrants out for our arrest. The licenses plates, registration and insurance are proper and in place. The only reason you stopped us is because we are black, in a white neighborhood at night."

The lead cop became irate told me not to talk to him in that tone and they were only doing their job.

I spoke. "What job? You stopped us for no reason. We didn't violate any traffic laws." I told him again "You only stopped us because we were black. And you know it!"

He and I both went at it verbally for a while longer. I then said "What do you plan to do? Beat four black high-school kids with a rubber hose for no reason?"

He was so angry I thought that he might actually try.

Finally, they cut us loose.

As I walked away the lead cop (with the big belly) called me back. He told me when I got out of highschool, I should think about becoming a cop.

A few minutes earlier I was mouthy and couldn't shut up. When he made that statement, I was speechless. He said you might catch a bullet but being a cop wasn't a bad job.

I said no thank you and walked away.

Cops, there is no explaining them. Yes, society needs them and, yes, they have a very hazardous job, but all too many of them become cops for the wrong reasons.

They received poor grades in highschool, have adrenaline

junkie personalities and are not here to serve and protect. In fact, all too many are racists and borderline sociopaths.

The Poem

In my freshman year I had an English teacher who instructed each student in the class to write a poem. Each of us was then required to read their poem aloud in front of the entire class. This is the poem I wrote and presented to my fellow students.

Poor little black boy who's just been born.
Poor little black boy all tired and worn.
Poor little black boy little knowing of the hate.
Poor little black boy that his color will create.
Poor little black boy all tired and worn.
Poor little black boy destined to be scorned.

Absolute silence. In the classroom there was absolute silence. The teacher then said, "Powerful."

I mentioned this poetic exercise because it caused me to think, and a fairly short time later the Creation Story originated.

The Creation Story

As a young man, the negative interaction with police and the overall tension between white and black races made me wonder about my life and our country.

This reflection also caused me to wonder. What does God think about racism? The following then came to me:

God viewed the expanse of nothingness and in his wisdom created the universe. He added the stars, moons, solar systems—Creation, as it came to be known.

However, God looked down from heaven and grew lonely.

Thus, he created two giants. One was white and one was black. These giants were magnificent mystical beings. They could fly through the air, swim to depths of the deepest oceans, possessed incredible strength.

Over time they created several intricate races of people, established monuments of great size, and were the authors of vast cities. They were truly mighty beings.

At some point in time, they became aware of their difference in skin color and animosity between them began. It festered and grew.

One day they had a set-to. They began to fight.

They were terrible in their rage. They destroyed all their cities, ruined the countries they created, murdered the masses without regard and, in an explosion of power, forfeited their very lives. Only rubble remained.

Buried beneath all the rubble lay these two giants, dead. Killed by the hatred of each other's skin color.

God looked down from heaven, and he realized that man his greatest creation was destroyed by his own hand.

And God cried!

I was sixteen when the above passage came to me. Once in later years while in college I recited the above story. People kept hounding me asking where did I read this? How did I find this?

No matter how I tried to explain it they didn't understand. When I wondered how God would react to the extreme racism in American this parable simply came to me in a flash. I didn't write it down; I didn't think about it. This "Creation Story" simply came to me in total.

At the time I was a sixteen-year-old sophomore in highschool.

Sports

While participating in athletics I heard all the usual clichés we have all heard before. You learn how to win and lose graciously, you learn more from losing than you do winning, you experience a sense of esprit de corps etc., etc.

The following is what I truly learned.

I was playing left Defensive End in a championship football game in high school. I received a blow to my head that gave me a concussion. I was knocked totally blind in my right eye. Still conscious but concussed in my right eye.

I quietly said to my defensive tackle I can't see out of my right eye. Let me know when the opponents are coming our way to which he agreed.

Fortunately, they didn't come our way for the next three plays. By the time there was a play heading in our direction the vision had returned to my eye.

Strangely neither one of us thought I should come out of the game due to the injury.

We also won the game.

Years later I was making a presentation in front a Board of high-powered individuals connected with the new Miller Park Baseball Stadium in Milwaukee, Wisconsin. One of my firm's duties was to ensure proper minority and women participation on the design portion of the project. The prime consultant to whom my firm reported didn't listen to me. They weren't timely enough to obtain the proper level of minority participation.

Even though I did determine how that level of participation could be achieved the Board was very cross with us/me and was letting me have it. Meanwhile the TV camera was 12 inches from my face.

I distinctly remember thinking despite the Board's harsh words no one was going to knock me blind in my right eye.

In time (with the support of a fine lady KM are her initials) our team met or exceeded our minority objectives in every category.

The point being there are times when I have found myself in a social setting that involved a verbal confrontation. However, if there isn't a credible threat of serious physical harm why be concerned. That's what I learned from playing contact sports.

A small point: Earlier I mentioned getting hit in my right eye in a rock fight. Years later in the football game described earlier I was knocked blind in my right eye. The sight returned but to this day my right eye is a little weaker than my left.

This is an example to me of how in life decisions can have a cumulative effect.

College

I graduated from high school in the upper one third of the 1,000 students in my class. That position coupled with my athletic achievements resulted in athletic college scholarships being offered to me.

I was offered a full wrestling scholarship at Northwestern University. I also was offered a full football scholarship at Syracuse University.

I desperately wanted to get away from Chicagoland so no Northwestern, and Syracuse, New York, was too far away.

A football coach suggested Ripon College in Ripon, Wisconsin. I went there and had four good years.

It was at Ripon that I first bought guns and learned how

to shoot. I enjoyed it and in later years I would go small game hunting.

At Ripon I truly became aware of how people viewed me and would continue to view me all my life. Everyone assumed I was a Physical Education major due to my athletic success. They were stunned to learn I majored in Economics.

People may not be stupid, but they are ignorant.

Hitchhiking

My senior year in high school I proposed to Mary, a classmate of mine. We agreed to wait until after college to finalize the marriage.

Mary as well other members of my graduating high school class attended an all-black college in Oklahoma.

I missed Mary, wanting to see her and my other friends in Oklahoma, but I had very little money.

Thus, I hitchhiked. I hit the road using my thumb. On my person was my switch blade and a sap (small pocket-sized black-jack) for protection.

I was able to pick up various rides from Wisconsin traveling to Oklahoma.

I managed to obtain rides until I was outside St. Louis, Missouri. It was here that a beater of a car carrying an old crone of a white woman and her husband, who was driving the car, stopped for me. I was sitting next to the woman.

That nasty old woman began stroking my penis. There is a line from the movie *48 Hours* starring Eddie Murphy where he is so horny, he states his "dick gets hard when the wind blows."

The wind wasn't blowing but to my horror I was becoming

aroused. I looked over at her husband who was driving the car with one hand and masturbating with the other.

I pushed her offending hand away and demanded they stop the car and let me out, now! They did and I sat on the road on top of the suitcase I was carrying seriously doubting this whole hitchhiking idea.

A few hours later night had fallen, and a car approached and slowed. The car then sped up aiming right for me.

I had to dive off the road into a ditch to avoid being run over. As it passed the passengers of the car a group of drunk white teenagers were laughing like crazy.

Fortunately, my luck changed. This was the year the World's Fair was in Canada. A man involved in the World's Fair picked me up and took me all the way from St. Louis to my destination in Oklahoma. He was a good man.

I arrived at my fiancée's room tired, dirty, and happy to see her.

The first thing she said was she wanted to break the engagement. This long-distance romance wasn't working. Further, the engagement ring on her finger hampered her ability to date.

Essentially Mary constituted my second Dear John letter (although delivered verbally).

I was hurt and stunned and realized I was a fool. I had no clue she felt this way. To see Mary, I had risked my life with teenage kids trying to run me down. More importantly I risked the integrity of my penis with that old crone.

I left my ex-fiancé and spent the night on a buddy's couch. The next day I began hitching back home. Heading to Chicago and then Evanston. A truck driver picked me up and took me several miles toward Chicago. He worked for a company that tested the metal strength of water towers worldwide.

He said in their firm once a year a man would by killed. He would slip off a water tower and die. This truck driver represented the second good man I met on this trip.

The next man that picked me up was relocating his farm from one state to another. As we drove, he would point out different soil types and what crops could be best grown in that soil.

He took me all the way to the South Side of Chicago. There I caught an L and went home to Evanston.

My mother was beyond angry with me when she found out I had hitched from Ripon, Wisconsin, to Oklahoma City, Oklahoma, and then back from Oklahoma to Chicago. I traveled roughly 2,000 miles round trip on my thumb. It took me days and there were times when I walked for miles.

On that trip I learned a lot about the world and myself.

In some ways I learned the most with the last truck driver who gave me a ride. The man who was moving his farm from one state to another. I asked him this question.

Why?

I was a young black man (who wasn't physically small) and it was night when he stopped to give me a ride.

Why did he stop for me?

He got a faraway look in his eyes, and he said, "I know what it's like to have your back against the wall and there is no one there to help."

Out of the multiple experiences I had in college that one conversation impacted me above all else.

That truck driver truly was a good man.

CHAPTER 12

Violence in College

The rest of my college years weren't particularly noteworthy in terms of violence. There were a few fist fights but nothing of note except for one situation.

I was dating a girl named Carol (whom I would later break up with) when it came to my attention that earlier in the day she had been in an argument with another student. The argument was with a man who disagreed with her political positions, and he did so in a loud aggressive manner in public.

He was a basketball player; Carol was petite and in this public setting he stood over her and began to berate her. I was off campus at the time.

I went to his dorm room and told him not to speak to her in that tone of voice. I didn't care whether he felt justified. He said, "I will talk to that broad any way I want."

I then chastised him for ignoring me while I was talking to him and said that he shouldn't take a nap during our discussion.

Then I understood. I had hit him, and he was face down on the floor. I used a left jab connecting with the bridge of his nose and he dropped. I swear I didn't realize I had thrown that punch.

Meanwhile his roommate who was watching this little

melodrama decided to attack me. His roommate had a Brown Belt in some type of martial art.

He could have used a Black Belt. What I did wasn't fancy. Bouncers have been using this technique for years. He rushed me. I simply took one step back and as he passed grabbed the back of his shirt with my left hand and back of his belt buckle with my right hand. I used his momentum to keep him moving quickly with my own weight and strength added to his movement. He hit the far wall headfirst and stayed still.

I looked at these two idiots and told them not to approach Carol again and they did not. Although at the time I was not entirely sure they heard me.

Two Men

There have been times in my life where I had to fight up to four men at once. This should never be one's first choice because it isn't fun at all.

However, there is a worse scenario and that's fighting two men. Not the type of knuckle heads mentioned above but men of a certain caliber.

I am referring to two men who are medium height, medium build but rawhide tough. Men who are physically strong but not from lifting weights. They are strong due to physical labor, i.e., construction workers.

These types of men can take a punch and deliver a blow and if they have been in many street fights together, they will know how to coordinate their attack.

These men have no fear.

Men of this type don't want to simply knock you down. They want to knock you down and then put their boots to you.

Should you have to fight men of this type, stick (punch) and move, stick, and move. Above all don't fall!

School Boy Grab the Gun

During the summer between high school and my first year in college I worked for the electric power company in Chicago. I obtained the job because that summer the power company's laborers were on strike.

This meant daily I ran the risks involved with crossing the strikers' picket line. Few people were willing to do so in Chicago. Those of us that did carry weapons in our trucks and always worked in pairs. Even still the tires on our personal cars were slashed and we endured other unpleasantries.

The next three summers I landed a job with a major Chicago based highway construction company. Part of the time I worked on an Asphalt Road Gang. The machine called a Barber Green would lay a six-foot-wide path of asphalt as we resurfaced Chicago's Dan Ryan express way. The more, narrow shoulders of the road needed to be completed by hand. I was part of the Road Gang who completed this task. Yes, that is what management called us, a Road Gang.

This company was my summer employer while in college. In addition to the asphalt work I dug ditches, swung a sledgehammer, and operated a handheld concrete saw.

However, most of the time I operated a jackhammer, breaking up concrete. The hammer weighed 90 pounds, the drill bit weighed 10 pounds, and the hose attached to the compressor weighed 30 pounds, for a total of 130 pounds. I worked that hammer 10 to 12 hours a day for six days a week, June, July, and August.

The work was hot and exhausting. The bosses would give the men salt tablets to push back the heat-related fainting spells.

My supervisors called a jackhammer "the gun." Because I was in college the men called me "Schoolboy."

At the start of most days my bosses would say, "Schoolboy, grab the gun."

They liked my work. So much so they tried to talk me into quitting college and working for this firm full time. The money was excellent, but the working conditions were brutal. One 15-minute break in the afternoon, a 30-minute lunch break. They did their best to start the lunch break late and further cheated the men by having us come back early.

I saw 45-year-old men who had been working there for a few years who looked as if they had seen 65 summers.

No, long term, this wasn't for me.

The breaking point for me was when a man on the crew was killed. We were working at night under the lights on a Chicago Expressway. As a crew we had worked 21 days in a row, 10 to 12 hours per day without a day off from work.

Construction sites are loud, jackhammers, bulldozers, trucks etc. One of the truck drivers was extremely tired, he was backing up his truck and the signaling device alerting all that a truck was in reverse malfunctioned.

A man digging a ditch didn't hear the truck coming. The truck ran him over killing him.

Our supervisors then decided we were tired and told us we had the following day off from work. The following day was a Sunday. A day we should have had off in the first place.

In the '60s and '70s, if you wanted to grow up fast, working on a road gang for a construction company in Chicago got the job done.

The Streets

After graduating from Ripon College in 1971 with a BA Degree in Economics I moved to Milwaukee, Wisconsin. A college friend of mine lived in Milwaukee. His name was McBride and I decided to relocate to this town. There was also another reason for moving to Milwaukee which I will discuss later.

While in Milwaukee I acquired a part-time job working for a program called Model Cities. I worked with Inner City businessmen and women to improve their operations. I also served as a tutor to Central City youth. As a tutor I came to realize different people had different measures for success. All of the youth we tutored were from the hood and many smoked. My superiors, as part of our educational teachings, wanted us to teach the kids certain "soft skills"; i.e., don't smoke cigarettes. It took a while but I finally got my superiors to understand at least the cigarettes had labels. In other words, getting the young bloods to stop smoking marijuana was a win.

Smoking marijuana would land them in jail but smoking cigarettes wouldn't.

Stop smoking dope, then we can work on dropping the habit of smoking all together. Take baby steps.

Milwaukee Streets

However, much of my time was running the streets with McBride and a few other brothers. Let me clarify. I wasn't gambling or using drugs or knocking over liquor stores.

However, it wasn't unusual for us to visit the basement of an acquaintance that contained racks of new clothing. This clothing had "fallen off the back of a truck."

We weren't involved in the highjacked truck it had nothing to do with us. Thus, it was fine if we purchased these goods at a steep discount. Our ages were early twenties, we were single, partied, and frequented inner-city nightclubs. It was the wild west and dangerously fun.

The music, the alcohol, the dancing, were wonderful. We would partake of fine food and even finer women. That lifestyle was (and still can be) very exciting, extremely seductive, and deadly.

There was an inner-city nightclub named Mr. J's that we would often visit.

One night McBride and I were in the club and a fight broke out ten feet in front of us. One man hit another. The man who received the blow came up slashing with a straight razor. While the man who threw the punch was weaving and evading the razor as best he could.

Then two bouncers arrived. One large black woman swinging her blackjack was yelling "Bobby, drop the knife." Even though this action was happening only a few feet from me, my immediate thought was "technically it's not a knife, it's a straight razor." I always had an eye for this type of detail.

To this day, I shave with a straight razor. A cutthroat razor truly gives the closest shave.

The police were called to Mr. J's, and we all scattered. Two weeks later McBride and I returned for another night out at Mr. J's. There were police cars everywhere.

Unbeknownst to us Mr. J's was having a private party that

night. A group of outsiders wanted into the party but were rejected.

The party crashers went to their cars and came back with guns. They began to fire into the club. Naturally the patrons of the club returned fire. It was a they blaze we blaze scenario.

Nine people were shot but here is the thing. In the middle of this firestorm one bouncer stood up and said, "Everyone stop shooting. We are all black people here." He was shot. Out of nine people hit with gun fire, he was the only one killed.

Proof again that death is capricious.

McBride and I ran the streets with guys named, JB, Henry Dent, Filthy Man, and Pretty Charlie. They were all characters. There was a prostitute that lived across the street. JB began dating her. I don't know about now but then it wasn't unusual for a working girl to have a boy friend. A non business sexual relationship, which was the situation with JB and the neighborhood hooker. One Saturday morning there was a loud banging on our door. When I opened the door JB was standing there in an agitated state. I knew he had spent the night with his girl friend from across the street and couldn't imagine why he was at our door so early in the morning.

JB blurted out "I have to use your bathroom." I said why not use your girlfriend's bathroom. He said and I quote, "I can't use her bathroom. She's nasty."

This woman was suitable enough for him to have sex with her throughout the night but she was too nasty for him to use her bathroom.

I laughed out loud as he pushed past me heading to our facilities. Then there was Filthy Man. He had that nickname because he would often step outside his marriage. In doing so over the course of four years he gave his wife gonorrhea five times. Pretty Charlie was so called because he was the ugliest motherfucker in America.

Truly.

Flawed characters one and all, but they were my friends. We were in our twenties, loved to party, loved the streets.

Mary Clayborne

We continued living this type of life for awhile. Then the following occurred.

There were four of us living together as roommates in a large rental house on Hampton Avenue. McBride, Henry Dent, Henry's girlfriend, Alice, and I lived in this home. The problem was, Henry was still legally married to a woman named Mary Clayborne who was the mother of his children.

Mary was a wildcat of a woman and one evening, apparently, she became fed up with the thought of her husband shacking up with another woman, Alice.

Mary rolled up to our house with her four brothers and the trunk of their car contained bricks.

Mary and her brothers began throwing bricks through the windows of our rental home. McBride, who was home yelled at them to stop. They kept throwing bricks.

It was then that McBride did something that changed our lives forever.

He grabbed a gun and shot Mary Clayborne.

He shot her in the head.

Damn!

What made it worse was when McBride came on the porch

with the gun Mary and her brothers upon seeing the gun jumped into their car and drove away.

McBride fired anyway with the bullet traveling through the rear window, hitting Mary in the head.

The only good news was McBride was using a 22-caliber rifle and not a more powerful weapon.

The 22-caliber slug was slowed by distance and again when it penetrated the back window of the car. The bullet lodged in her skull but didn't penetrate Mary's brain.

Mary didn't die.

I wasn't there at the time of the shooting. I was somewhere else doing something else. I arrived two days later, and I found out what had transpired.

I went into overdrive.

The police arrested McBride but before I saw him in jail, I needed to do something else first.

Henry and I went to the hospital to see Mary, his wife. This woman was not only angry but filled with hate. Henry did the talking, attempting to smooth things over. I was there only to have her understand that, yes, this was a tragedy, but it ended here.

She, her brothers, and the rest of her kin were not to attempt retaliation against McBride, his family or me.

It was a message she didn't want to hear but even in her agitated state she knew my position was sound.

I also felt in a strange way she was embarrassed. She allowed herself to get shot. What did she think was going to occur when she attacked our home? If she had been killed who was going to raise her kids? It was obvious Henry wasn't up to the task. He'd already bailed on their relationship when he took up with Alice.

Next, I had to contact family and friends to raise the funds for McBride's bail. We were able to get him released once the bail was set and paid.

I remember walking into the jail's official area for such things and slowing counting out several thousand dollars in cash.

Strangely, none of the officials asked me where I could acquire that much cash on relatively short notice.

Then I spearheaded the effort to raise money for his attorney.

The interaction with Mary and her family ended regarding this event.

However, the system wasn't finished with this event, or us.

In time, McBride was tried in court and the judge sentenced him to prison. He was in prison for years. He did time, hard time, at the Green Bay Correctional Institution a Maximum-Security prison.

I would visit him often over those years. I won't go into detail, but it was a horrible experience for him and not very good for me either.

Earlier I stated there was another reason for me relocating to Milwaukee after graduating from Ripon.

In my senior year at Ripon, I applied to and was accepted into the Master of Business Administration (MBA) programs at Northwestern University, Miami of Ohio at Oxford, and Marquette University.

I chose Marquette and moved to Milwaukee. I was working on my MBA. I had a work study scholarship under the Model Cities program while at Marquette.

When Marquette found out about my involvement in the shooting of Mary, two things happened. The police interest in me evaporated. I believe Marquette "white peopled" that whole thing and encouraged the police to lose interest in me. Marquette didn't want to be anywhere near a crime of this type.

The second thing they did was kick me out of their MBA program.

I wasn't in the home for the shooting, but I did live in the home and the lease was in my name.

One other point. McBride shot Mary with *my* gun.

CHAPTER 13

Afterwards

WHILE MCBRIDE WAS INSIDE, I WORKED WITH A GROUP THAT enrolled him in a master's degree in a Social Work program at University of Wisconsin–Milwaukee, which he completed through the mail. Upon his release he continued his studies and earned his master's degree as a Social Worker. He became very active working within Milwaukee's Inner City. Over the years he made a significant, positive difference.

Due to his successful efforts at improving Milwaukee's Inner City, a group of people (I had only a very small part in this) were able to lobby Wisconsin Governor Tony Earl to pardon McBride.

He received his pardon and continued as a stellar citizen.

McBride changed for the good and so did I. No more nightclubs for me. I settled down and got married and had two sons.

Also, I met someone who was an officer at the then First Wisconsin National Bank and was offered a position in their Management Training program.

To the East

It was during the dark days when McBride was in prison that we developed the phrase "To the East."

It's what we would say at the end of an in-person visit, or the end of a phone call. In later years we would also close emails with this phrase.

It didn't have a religious connotation. We didn't mean to face the east in prayer; it simply meant today wasn't a good day and at times an awful day.

However, tomorrow might be better. So, in the morning look to the East and watch the sun rise.

It's a new day and maybe a better day.

The Bank

After a few years at the bank, I was promoted to Assistant Manager of the Teutonia and Capital Drive Branch.

One day we were hit by bank robbers. Two men, black, entered the bank. One man placed a pistol to the back of the head of the bank's elderly security guard. The outlaw told him if he had been wearing a gun, he would have killed him. Instead, the robber kept the gun alongside his head but pointed the barrel toward the ceiling and squeezed the trigger, firing the gun, as he pushed the guard to the floor.

His partner in crime then entered the bank waving a shotgun.

The first outlaw vaulted the teller's cage and began stuffing cash into a bag. The bag he was using was a paper bag. In his haste he stepped on the bag it ripped open and much of the cash was dumped on to the floor.

These guys were clowns, but the guns made them extremely dangerous clowns.

There was an addition to the drama. When the outlaw ripped the bag one of our younger tellers gave a nervous giggle. Not the best thing to do.

The branch manager and I had taken cover behind our desks. As luck would have it, I made eye contact with the outlaw holding the shotgun. He said, "You pressed the silent alarm, didn't you." I said, "No, I didn't." Although we both knew that I had done so.

We began to argue: yes you did, no I didn't.

As they left the bank, Mr. Shotgun fired the shotgun over my desk. If I had been standing the blast would have taken me in the face.

They then ran out the door.

Two thoughts entered my mind. First, I was relieved no one was seriously injured. Second, I couldn't believe after all the nonsense I had live through growing up in Chicagoland I almost got shot in the face while working as an officer at a bank!

One other point. This was an Inner City Bank Branch with primarily black clients and employees. On the day of the robbery, we did have a few white people in the branch either as customers or staff.

When the pistol shot was fired, the white people were looking around, saying, "What was that noise?"

Every single black person in the bank knew exactly what caused the noise and we hit the floor.

This might be comical to some, but to me it was a sobering reminder of the profound differences in our society regarding black and white experiences.

After a few more years I attained the position of Vice President-Manager of the National Division. I had five junior officers reporting to me. The National Division made loans to primarily Fortune 500 Companies.

My people and I traveled to New York, calling on American Express, JC Penny, Woolworth, etc. We also traveled to the West

Coast and Pacific Northwest to call on such firms as Mattel, the Carnation Company, and Weyerhaeuser.

We would meet with the corporate CFOs of these companies, selling them cash management services and making loans to their organizations.

My authority was such I could make a $2.5 million loan solely on my signature. My boss and I with our two signatures could lend up to $5 million without Loan Committee approval.

I still consider myself a banker by trade.

Every year my division would bring in more revenue than established in the annual budget with less expense.

I/we were good at our jobs.

At the bank I learned how a company works and what contributes to success or failure. I also learned events in the marketplace could adversely affect a business. Often the business had no control over these events; i.e., recessions, inflation, monetary policy, and or fiscal policy.

More importantly, at the bank I continued to learn about people. For example, once I was told one of my Fortune 500 clients didn't appreciate having a black man as his banker making in-person calls to his office.

Then he said, "But at least he is a man." A woman banker as his contact would have been even worse. This racist, misogynistic jerk was my client; he was also the bank's client, which meant I was powerless to change this situation.

However, I let it be known I wasn't happy.

The other aspect of our bank (all major banks at the time) was "redlining." Basically, there were certain lenders at the bank who wouldn't make a car loan or home loan to people that lived within a certain zip code.

Or if the loan was made, it was at a higher rate due to the perceived additional risk. I hit the roof over that one. Unfortunately, I only achieved modest success in terms of changing the bank's redlining policy.

As I said earlier, I have never been impressed with the race of mankind.

As time went on, I became involved with the Northcott Neighborhood House located in Milwaukee, Wisconsin. The mission of this non-profit organization was to assist and support underprivileged inner-city children and their families. One Christmas I decided to assist this organization by delivering toys to them for these children. Free of charge.

As stated, Mattel was one of my clients and I had become very familiar with their operation. Mattel spent a tremendous amount of time developing prototypes of dolls and other toys.

They would then test these toys in real life settings observing children as they played, (or didn't play) with a given toy. The toys that failed these tests weren't going to market and would be discarded.

These prototype toys were brand new, in excellent condition but for some reason the children didn't take to them as eagerly as Mattel would have hoped.

I approached my contact at Mattel and explained that I wanted them to sell these toys to me at a discount. I would personally pay the cost and would also pay for the shipping.

Once Mattel understood the toys were headed for inner city youth, they gave these toys to me at no cost. They even paid for the shipping.

They were a fine company and extremely gracious.

Because of logistical problems and lack of space at Northcott

I had the toys (Mattel gave me a number of toys) shipped to First Wisconsin shortly before Christmas. I then had them secured in one of the bank's storage rooms.

Word leaked out that I had control of a mountain of toys. Some, not all, Vice Presidents and Assistant Vice Presidents began asking me to give them some of these toys for free, for their children.

These men could more than afford to buy toys for their children.

I was beyond angry and told them no. This was not what they wanted to hear.

They then tried to go around me and retrieve toys from the storage area.

Because I am who I am I placed these toys under the lock and key of several of the banks security guards all of whom were black men.

I explained to them these toys were for Northcott Neighborhood House Inner-City youth and no one but me was authorized to move these items.

These greedy bank officers were stunned and angry when neither the guards nor I would relent.

Northcott received the toys, and I received a black eye in the minds of some of my peers. Remember, in time these Vice Presidents were going to be Senior Vice Presidents and Executive Vice Presidents.

I want to emphasize that most of the employees at First Wisconsin were fine people. Many have gone on to play a positive role in our society.

However, given how I was mentally wired, there were certain policies, events that I couldn't tolerate.

This meant in time I had to leave.

After twelve years at the bank, I resigned.

When I announced my resignation, bank senior management wanted me to remain. I was told in time I could become an Executive Vice President.

Perhaps, but the negative events mentioned above coupled with my entrepreneurial mindset meant managing my own shop was where I needed to be.

I left the bank and formed one small company after another until Jane, my wife, and I established our current firm, American Design, Inc., 31 years ago. With her help the business is a success.

Violence: "Once More unto the breach" (William. Shakespeare, Henry V, Act III, Scene I)

Jane and I live in a beach community in San Diego that becomes very crowded on the 4th of July. About twenty years ago, when I was in my late fifties, a group of 12 men gathered in front of our home. They had been drinking heavily and created a serious disturbance to which I responded.

Of the twelve men four of them broke away. They threw two hands full of firecrackers at the feet of a 10-year-old girl who happened to be standing nearby.

When these mini-bombs exploded the little girl screamed. To this day I can close my eyes and hear her scream.

Eight of the men ran past me followed by the four attackers of this child. I was sitting in a courtyard adjacent to the sidewalk where they were running.

I didn't say a word. I simply attacked the four. I hit one man in the chest knocking him flat, the second was a left jab to the bridge of his nose he went down quickly. The third I simply grabbed as he rushed me and threw him into the wall of the next-door building.

The fourth man got behind me. He was shorter than I but wide and very strong. He picked me up as if I were a 10-year-old child. This man had me in a bear hug lifted me off my feet and he slammed us both to the concrete sidewalk.

I told you earlier fighting four men is no fun.

As I was flying through the air with his arms wrapped around me in a bear hug, I relaxed, saving my energy. In this type of situation, no matter how tight the grip of the attacker when both men crash to the ground a slight space is created between the two bodies.

I used a wrestling move called an inside switch. I timed it so that upon impact I drove my left elbow between the man and myself. Used my upper body strength to push him a way with my left arm. However, at the last second once he was at arm's length, I grabbed his shirt with my left hand and pull him toward me, hitting him with a right hook that landed in his eye.

I hit him so hard he bounced away from me. So, I rushed him grabbed his shirt again with my left and began beating him with my right fist.

I say fist. Please understand a fist isn't a fist. It is a hammer. You can kill a man with a hammer if you aren't careful.

Jane had witnessed the entire event and she yelled, "John!" I then came to my senses and let him go. The eight men who ran away returned not to fight but to retrieve their four fallen comrades.

When I get in these situations there is tremendous anger in my gut, but my mind is clear.

I am not in my right mind. It's almost an out-of-body experience.

I never worry about a confrontation with police, or what I will tell the judge, or being sued or sustaining injuries of my own. There is only the action.

Until the police sirens, or in this case my wife yelling my name, causes me to "wake up" and return to the present.

I was in my fifties when this event occurred. You would think by that point in time I would have changed.

An oddity. After this fight and back in our home I asked Jane to check my back for knife wounds. At times after a street fight you are still standing feeling victorious. Without knowing or feeling a knife wound in your back. You think you have won only to be bleeding to death internally. The pain masked by the adrenalin flying through your body.

Jane looked at me as if to say what kind of man did, I marry but she did check, and no wounds were discovered.

Here is the oddity. Jane kept saying I could have killed someone. She wasn't concerned about my well being only that I might have caused the death of another.

Odd.

It should be noted the police did arrive taking notes as they spoke with me and others who had witnessed the fight.

When I explained these men had assaulted a 10-year-old girl with a series of firecrackers, the officer stopped writing. He then said, "Sometimes there is street justice."

Both police officers then left with no more involvement with me.

It Will Make a Man Out of You

During my childhood, anytime I faced duress my mother or grandmother or Big Momma would say it will make a man out of you. The brutally cold Chicago winters, the early morning paper route seven days a week, fights, all of it.

There were times I felt the events of this nature went too far. I was nine years old, and I would often go fishing with Grandma and Big Momma. My mother didn't like to fish but the three of us did. We would leave early in the morning heading to "the river" to fish.

One morning my grandmother was driving her beater of a car. I was in the back seat with Big Momma who decided to open a thermos bottle of hot coffee for a drink.

At that moment Grandma hit a pothole that caused the car to jump which in turn caused Big Momma to splash scalding hot coffee on my lap.

To make matters worse I had fallen asleep. When the hot coffee hit me, I screamed and leapt straight up in the air hitting my head on the roof of the car, hard.

They laughed. In fact, Grandma was laughing so hard she almost lost control of the car.

"Don't worry, Johnny. It will make a man out of you."

CHAPTER 14

Not so Remarkable?

I WAS AN EXCELLENT WRESTLER IN HIGH SCHOOL. I WAS ALL AREA and All State Offensive Guard in football in the state of Illinois. Also, in my senior year the coaches were going give me my own Lacrosse Team. I would be a Captain. I had academic success as well. I graduated in the upper one-third of my class. I am in the Ripon College Athletic Hall of Fame for wrestling and football.

In addition, I put myself through college. I managed the entire process of obtaining teachers' recommendations, completing all the forms needed to gain admittance as well as forms for financial aid and work study. I worked, had scholarships and I paid every dime of my college cost. Perhaps that isn't so remarkable, others have done it.

However, I would also send a check home every month to support Mom and Jesse. Often people send money to their kids when the child is in college. Not with me. It was the opposite.

When I was sixteen, I told Mom, "I am going to college."

She said, "How are you going to get there?"

I said, "I don't know but I will think of something."

In later years I asked Mom why she seemed surprised that I decided to go to college. What did she think I was going to do, was my question.

She said, "I thought you would get out of high school and get a job."

As I thought about her answer, I realized during all my years in school neither Mom nor Jesse every attended a teacher-parent conference. They didn't join the PTA. They never said, "Johnny, have you done your homework?"

How could they? Mom had an eighth-grade education and Jesse couldn't read or write.

Teachers intimidated them.

I wasn't bringing the police to their door. I hadn't gone to Juvenile Reform School. I was sharing my paper route money with them, and no teachers were contacting them saying I was ditching classes.

That was a win.

I accomplished all of this because my upbringing made a man out of me.

Maybe they were correct.

However, even if they were correct, I didn't want my two sons to have my childhood. Not even close.

My Sons

In high school I knew, I simply knew, I would get married, have two sons, not daughters. The names of my first-born son would be Ryan and my younger son Scott.

This is exactly what happened. Ryan Williams and Scott Williams, my sons, are good men. The bulk of their childhood was spent in Mequon, Wisconsin, an upscale suburb of Milwaukee, Wisconsin.

There were many times when I would visit Mom and Jesse in Evanston and take my sons with me. I wanted my sons to see where I came from, to meet some of my more outrageous relatives and obtain a taste of my earlier life.

Once and only once did I take them to ETHS. I wanted them to see my high school athletic trophies that were still on display and meet some of the people still employed at the school who knew me.

When I was inducted into the Ripon College Athletic Hall of Fame, I had my sons attend the ceremony with me simply to give them additional insight into my past life. In college I was All Conference in football, All Conference in Wrestling and had a wrestling record of 59-3-1. My wrestling weight class was 190 lbs. A major sportswriter claimed I was one of the best light-heavyweight wrestlers in the nation.

My opinion of my ability in this area wasn't so much that I was an excellent wrestler. I was simply pretty good in a fight.

I wasn't attempting to impress my sons with my past accomplishments. I wanted them to understand, if possible, why I was the way I was.

Scott was a fine athlete who played football at Homestead High School in Mequon. Scott did play one year of football for UW Madison. He then decided to retire from the sport to focus on his academic achievement. Scott graduated from UW Madison in four years. He currently is employed with a successful Silicon Valley-based firm. Scott has a way of making positive things happen at his firm.

Ryan was also a fine athlete who played football at Homestead High School. Ryan attended Yale University. Ryan played football his first year there and then retired from the sport. His academic achievement was outstanding. Ryan received his undergraduate degree from Yale University and went on to obtain his law degree from Georgetown University.

Ryan is a tenured law professor at the Thomas R. Kline School of Law of Duquesne University in Pittsburgh.

Both of my sons are good men and good citizens.

Fatherhood

My ex-wife, the mother of my sons, was/is a good mother. She is a member of Mensa, with a genius IQ. Presently she is retired but spent her career as an attorney in Milwaukee.

Her background is German/English, and she is a direct descendent of President John Adams. In fact, she can trace her ancestors all the way back to William the Conquer.

Her family were members of the upper echelons of Milwaukee society. In short, my sons are descendants of presidents and slaves.

I divorced my wife due in part to a fundamental difference in our philosophy of life. It became evident she believed with all her heart in the law.

I never did. I have always believed in justice. These are often two completely different concepts.

I love my sons more than my own life. However, I decided early on I wasn't going out drinking with them. We didn't hang out. I wasn't their best friend.

I was their father.

As their father, I taught them certain things. Keep your word, don't back down from a confrontation and don't make promises you can't keep.

I taught them practical skills i.e., how to shoot a gun, box, drive a car, carve a turkey and deal with people.

In addition, I explained to my sons, be very careful about the people you call friends. I have very few friends, but they are all good people. Friends from high school: Guy Ward, Bill Campbell, Fred Wharton, and John Powers. Friends from college: Terry Capes, Jeff Trickey, Tom Bachhuber.

And more recently:

Roger "RK" Kay, author, sailor, movie director, some say a genius, and a man for all seasons.

Robert Thele and Miriam Cisco excellent businesspeople who are always on the right side of history.

Kristine Martinsek gifted at organization and a woman who has truly helped the City of Milwaukee and me.

J Allen Stokes another instrumental person in the support of Milwaukee and me. Stokes has also been my friend and confidant for over fifty years.

Errol Barnett is a clear thinker, highly intelligent, loyal to his family, his friends, and the best pure banker that I have ever met.

They are talented, gifted, honest, industrious people one and all, and the best of the group is my wife, Jane.

In the course of time, I remarried.

My wife is an attractive, wonderful, intelligent person with two sons of her own from a previous marriage, but more about Jane later.

All four boys know each other and get along well.

In preparation for our wedding, I felt something was needed. On an individual basis I brought each of our sons to Mark Berman & Son, a well-known upscale men's clothing company in Mequon, Wisconsin.

I wanted them to know how to dress properly as a gentleman in our society.

Along with two tailors from Berman's I showed the boys how to select a 100 percent light wool fabric for their tailor-made suits. This type of suit keeps a man warm in the winter and cooler in the summer.

Their tailor-made shirts were 100 percent white Egyptian cotton with their initials embossed, white on white, on the cuffs. This type of fabric allows the shirt to breathe.

The tie was 100 percent silk and the tip of the tie, if red let's say, matched the burgundy belt. The belt in turn matched the burgundy dress shoes. All of which were accented by original cuff links with flecks of red.

This how a man in business should dress.

I believe a man's sons should be able to handle a physical or verbal fight, dining in an upscale restaurant in Downtown Chicago, attending a function at Carnegie Hall New York City, or trap shooting at a gun range in Eagle, Wisconsin.

He knows how to dress the part for each situation and how to carry himself no matter the occasion.

This skill set will make men out of a man's sons.

Note: I taught both Ryan and Scott gun safety. After the gun safety lessons, I took them trap shooting at the McMiller Sports Center. This facility is managed by Wisconsin's Department of Natural Resources.

Scott was eight years old, and Ryan was ten when we three began trap shooting together.

Both boys were very good shots. However, they never wanted to go squirrel, rabbit or pheasant hunting with me.

They enjoyed shooting but didn't want to hunt. Their position was neither right nor wrong they simply had no desire to kill.

It's not odd simply a different mindset from my own.

I mentioned earlier I still shave with a cutthroat razor.

Admittedly one can seriously injury oneself if you don't know what you are doing.

Twice, I offered to teach Ryan and Scott how to shave with a razor of this type. I told them I wanted to pass on this skill while my hands were still steady.

As with hunting they both declined.

For some reason their decision regarding the cutthroat razor left me a little sad.

However, on balance my relationship with my sons is excellent and one that I cherish. Many years ago, when the boys were still in high school, we were out for supper. Ryan and Scott were talking between the two of them about what traits they had learned from their father. I was there but they were speaking to each other as if I wasn't present.

Scott said he learned from Dad, "You keep going, you keep going, you never quit, you never give up."

Ryan then said, "Yes and you do the right thing."

Nothing in my life has filled me with greater joy than hearing those unsolicited words from my two sons. That told me I was completing my mission as their father. Overhearing that conversation was a joy and a win!

Jane, My Wife

My wife is Jane Jonas Williams. I call her Lady Jane. We have been married for over 25 years, and she has been a blessing to my life. Jane was born and raised in Milwaukee, Wisconsin. She has nine brothers and sisters. Jane's parents had ten children. A good Irish Catholic family. I find it faintly amusing that the birth of her siblings was boy, girl, boy, girl, etc. for a total of ten children, always alternating. Perhaps, this was her parents' idea of planned parenting.

Jane is a woman who is very intelligent, works hard to maintain her physical being, is passionate, and has a high level of integrity.

Jane has worked with me in establishing multiple businesses over the years with our current firm having achieved a significant degree of success. In large part due to Jane's support and commitment.

She has supported me in some very dark days of my life, assisted me daily in the care of my 96-year-old mother, and Jane still finds time to provide emotional support for her siblings and children.

Jane is a positive force in the community and never says no to someone in need.

Much of my success and happiness over the last few decades is due to Jane's love and support.

Also, after all this time, Jane still makes me laugh.

Yes, I love her, but I also like her.

Lady Jane makes me be a better me.

Bottom line, she is the kind of woman who makes a man stay home at night.

My ID (persona)

The upbringing that I had has created a man who believes strongly in pride, honor, and justice. More than once, I have helped someone less fortunate than I. At times at some physical risk to me personally.

There is no death wish contained in my psyche. However, I believe how a man lives his life is important.

Not for how long.

I enjoy spending time with my family, my wife, and our sons and the few people I call friends. A few men and even fewer women but I do appreciate these relationships.

Mental and physical exercise is important, and spending time alone is good with me.

To be liked is fine, to be loved is permissible however, above all I would rather be respected.

I remember with pride my athletic and academic achievements, a certain amount of success in business, with the assistance of others. I am also proud that I paid for my ex-wife's three years of law school at Marquette University. Further I paid for all four years of Ryan and Scott's undergraduate degrees and assisted Ryan with funding his three years at Georgetown Law.

Luke is Jane's younger son, and I paid for his Undergraduate Degree in Architecture at the University of Minnesota.

Luke is an architect in Minnesota and Jane's oldest (Jonas) is a Registered Nurse in San Diego and, yes, I assisted financially in his higher education as well. As a nurse he is on the front lines fighting Covid-19 and other deadly diseases every day.

These are two fine men.

I call our four sons the Fantastic Four.

Basically, there is a certain amount of pride in what I have accomplished in my life. At times I had assistance but often I did not.

However, these days I all too often remember my failures. As a student I shouldn't have had that relationship with a high-school teacher. Obviously, she had a problem.

I never should have kept a loaded gun in the house around McBride. I knew his, and my, temperament.

I was dismissed from the MBA program at Marquette

University. Running the streets was in my blood and I couldn't put that lifestyle behind me fast enough.

In this instance I showed a true lack of control and depth of character.

Yes, I received my Undergraduate Degree in Economics from Ripon College. I also obtained a Graduate Degree in Banking through the Stonier School of Banking from Rutgers University. In addition, I received a Management in Business Degree from the Kellogg School of Management through Northwestern University.

Nevertheless, my failure with Marquette to this day truly hurts. I only have myself to blame

Understanding my multiple failures I have embraced the concept of *Nunc Coepi*, which means "Now I begin." Perhaps, a deeper meaning is "Now I begin to start anew." This I have attempted with my life. Despite my failures and inadequacies I have attempted to better myself and move forward.

End Game

I know next to nothing about my sire's side of the family. However, the people on my mother's side of the family have faith. Part of our oral family history states Jane Holmes, my Great-grandmother's, grandmother, the slave, would take a walk every morning. One morning she stayed in bed and sent for all her children, grandchildren, and great grandchildren. When they were assembled by her bed she said, "I am going home." Then she died. She was over 100 years old.

In my family when it's time to die we simply go to sleep.

My grandmother (Viola) told my mother's sister, "I am going

home." That night my Grandmother Viola died in her sleep. She was 101-years old.

My mom always had me in her corner and we both fought this thing called life. On January 21, 2022, at 4:30 a.m. at age 96 my mother died.

Her fight ended. As she passed, I whispered to her, "Mom, I love you, and I will see you on the other side."

I shall always remember my Great-aunt Sarah who handled her end game with grace and style.

One day she said to me, "Johnny, I never did have children, and I have outlived two husbands. It is time for me to get on away from here."

I said, "Auntie, you have many more years to live. She looked at me and said, "I didn't come here to stay. I will go home to my Father's House."

Four weeks later she was dead. Auntie said goodbyes, cleaned up her few financial affairs and went to sleep.

I think about my life, both the good and the bad, my misdeeds, mistakes, and my careless acts of kindness. As I enter the winter of my years, I wonder.

When this struggle is over, will I be confined to Dante's Ninth Circle?

Or will he understand my attempt to start anew and allow me to enter my *Father's House?*

—John (JT) Williams

www.ingramcontent.com/pod-product-compliance
Lightning Source LLC
Chambersburg PA
CBHW051211120626
46547CB00013B/1310